graphic interiors

spaces designed by graphic artists

corinna dean

ROCKPORT PUBLISHERS

First published in the United States of America by
Rockport Publishers, Inc.
33 Commercial Street
Gloucester, Massachusetts 01930-5089
Telephone: (978) 282-9590
Facsimile: (978) 283-2742
www.rockpub.com

ISBN 1-56496-674-7

10 9 8 7 6 5 4 3 2 1

Art Directon: Stephen Perfetto
Design: Madison Design
Cover Image: Mike Tonkin

Printed in China

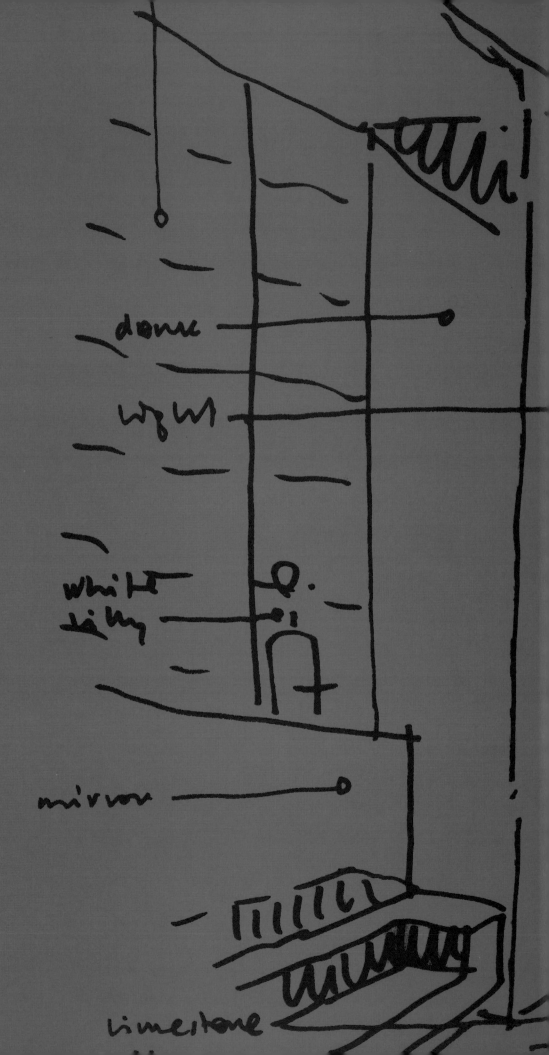

EATING.

contents

Introduction

10
Tonkin Architects with
Hybrid Graphic Designs
Project: Tong Zhi Karaoke Bar, Hong Kong
Project: Yuen Long Cinema, Hong Kong
Project: Flex Bar, Hong Kong
Project: Mong Kok Cinema, Hong Kong

24
Ben Kelly Design Studio
With Lippa Pearce Design
Project: Halfords Store, Sheffield & Swansea, England
With Assorted Images; Tim Head & Charlie Hood, Artists
Project: Children's Gallery, National Museum of Science &
Industry, London

40
Graven Images
Project: Room at the Top, Glasgow, Scotland
Project: Tun Ton, Bathgate, Scotland
Project: Favorit, Edinburgh, Scotland

60
FAT
Project: Kesselskramer Office, Amsterdam

70
Pentagram
With James/Snow and The Alliance
Minnesota Children's Museum, Minneapolis

78
Met Design Studio
Project: Wired Worlds—Exploring the Digital Frontier Gallery,
The National Museum for Photography, Film and Television

88
24/seven
With BCD
Project: The Bar at ICA, London
Project: Klinik Hairdresser, London

100
The Designers Republic
Branson Coates Architecture
Project: Moshi Moshi Sushi, London

110
System Typography Integrated Programme (STIP)
Project: PTT Post Buildings, Holland

120
Orb Design Studio
Project: Kreuzberg Apartment, Berlin

130
Softroom
Kielder Belvedere, Northumberland, England
Swiss Army Knife House

144
Traast and Gruson
Project: Signs in the Street Exhibition
Milan Triennial 1992 Exhibition
Project: Death Made Tangible Exhibition, Museum of the
Hague, Amsterdam

156
General Lighting & Power
Project: Greenwich Meridian Time, Greenwich, England

166
Marc Newson Ltd with Richard Allen
Project: Private Jet

170
Imagination
The Journey Zone, The Dome, London

180
Navyblue.com and Katy Ghahremani
and Michael Kohn
Hanger House™

189
Directory of Firms

191
Author's Note

Jean Luc Godard's cult film *Alphaville* demonstrates the powerful role played by graphics and architecture to evoke a specific sense of place. In Godard's *Alphaville*, a futuristic dystopian metropolis is portrayed using the backdrop of '60s Paris. Godard focuses in on typographical symbols, the type favored by pop artists: arrows, luminescent numbers, and neon street signs flashing with hypnotic rhythm against a screen of high-rise tower blocks. The film is an example of the parallel role that the two creative forms—architecture and graphics—play in creating a visual language to represent the essence of an age.

As the production of contemporary graphics extends beyond the static form to the application of digital graphics, the production of architecture in contrast is primarily rooted to a specific location. Despite this difference, both disciplines are being rocked by the digital revolution. But it can be argued that graphic designers react more quickly to their cultural surroundings as the process of production is more rapid, from concept to finished product. In turn, architecture, in which the terms of production are far lengthier, reacts slower to the cultural fabric. What happens when the two disciplines of architecture and graphic design meet head on?

Increasingly, multidisciplinary practices are applying their acquired knowledge to other areas of design, leading to a breakdown of conventional design paradigms. As a response to this reappraisal of design professions, educational institutions are broadening design curriculum to encompass a cross-fertilization of disciplines. Leading the crossover is the consumer impresario Phillipe Starck. From toothbrushes to flat pack blueprints for DIY houses, Starck applies his hand to design, unrestricted by categorization. And before him came Archigram, Archizoom, the Deutsche Werkbund, and the De Stijl, to name a few groups who formed loose movements forged under a design treatise to produce works executed in a variety of media.

Graphic Interiors sets out to examine some of these issues through a selection of projects that illustrate collaborations between graphic designers and architects and the work of multidisciplinary practices.

When considering graphics as the application of text and symbols to a building in order to communicate a system of information or beliefs, one can look as far back as to the thirteenth century for examples. The great medieval cathedrals such as Chartres, Salisbury, and Canterbury are adorned with gargoyles applied to ward off evil spirits and religious iconography to represent biblical beliefs. Later, the importance of graphic design—albeit during the process stage—was promulgated through Andrea Palladio's *Four Books on Architecture*, published in 1570. Illustrated with examples of the classical orders, Palladio stressed the importance of drawing and the graphic representation of architecture.

introduction

With the acceleration of the Industrial Revolution at the turn of the nineteenth century, companies were beginning to realize the power of corporate identity. Germany's growing industrial base was epitomized in companies such as the German electricity supplier, AEG, which commissioned Peter Behrens, a member of the Deutsche Werkbund, to create an identity that could be applied across the board, from the company's graphics and product design right through to the architecture of the factory complex.

The Dutch De Stijl movement, formed in 1918, was exemplary in its cross-fertilization of ideas that brought together an array of artists, poets, and architects. Its three core members—painters Piet Mondrian and Theo van Doesburg and architect Gerrit Rietveld—were concerned with the application of art and culture to the composition of built environments with the idea of liberating art from the cult of the individual. Using a limited palette of primary colors to emphasize the structural elements of design, the project that best manifested these ideas was the Cafe L'Aubette in Strasbourg, Germany, completed in 1928. Working closely with the architects, a group of artists designed an integrated composition of graphics and space using color and light to produce abstract wall reliefs.

At the latter part of the twentieth century a reaction against modernism manifested itself in many counter movements and styles. Robert Venturi and Denise Scott-

Brown's book *Learning from Las Vegas*, published in 1972, lamented the decorated shed as a building type worthy of architectural consideration. The book's premise states that the billboard-clad buildings that line the Las Vegas strip represent a manifestation of the economic market that is a driving factor in informing architectural design.

Then came the rise of Post Modernism with its main theorists stating that a building's façade is a representation of its semiotic properties and that its materials and forms are loaded with historical and cultural references. Michael Graves' Portland Public Services Building in Portland, Oregon (1980-82), combines Art Deco elements with classical motifs dividing the skyscraper's façade into three classical orders of the base, shaft, and capital.

With the increasing number of megalopolises rising out of the Pacific Rim, cities such as Taipei, Shanghai, and Seoul, are emerging as organic hybrids. Urban landscapes made up of neon signs, billboards, and advertising screens culminate in a plethora of messages and signs that reduce the city to a chaotic hub of consumer exchange.

Four artists who can be loosely grouped together for their use of text and language to blur the distinctions between private and public space are Jenny Holzer, Lawrence Weiner, Barbara Krueger, and Joseph Kossuth. Jenny Holzer creates text-based LED pieces and places them in public sites such as Times Square in New York and Leicester Square in London, juxtaposing her plain speaking art with advertising screens. Her work questions what is deemed acceptable in private spaces but not public and how we interpret text according to which medium is used to convey the words. These artists have proven the powerful effect that text has when taken out of its normal context and used for polemical reasons, especially within technologies used by the mass media.

Some examples of architects who have integrated text-based pieces into their work are Massimiliano Fuksas, Jean Nouvel, and Herzog and De Meuron. Herzog and De Meuron's work articulates the façade as a conveyor of ephemeral messages, a negation of the period when architecture was rooted in a sense of place. The façade mediates as an information screen and is often inscribed with text as an acknowledgment of the growing information highway.

This short introduction illustrates the varied and long relationship graphic design has had to architecture. In the current climate it is undeniable that the two areas of design—architecture and graphics—meet head on with the advent of digital technology, an integral design tool for many practices. Graphic designers can try out their work in the three-dimensional sphere with the use of modeling programs and architects can experiment with desktop publishing programs, as well as the aforemen-

tioned modeling programs developed for animation and filmic special effects. As the digital revolution gathers pace, questions are inevitably being thrown up as to what these cyberspaces will look like and who will be designing them.

Fuelled by interactive web computer games and the evolution of design communities in cyberspace, the enormous repercussions in terms of how architecture is viewed and designed are coming to light. The Designers Republic, graphic designers who collaborated on the Moshi Moshi Sushi restaurant in London together with Branson Coates Architects (illustrated in Chapter Eight), are increasingly moving into the arena of computer game design, creating three-dimensional environments and branding for games companies such as Sony. With the development of these tools and animation software, space visualization and programming will no longer be in the hands of architects but whoever is able to design digital environments.

General Lighting and Power, the digital designers who created the Greenwich Meridian Time project (illustrated in Chapter Thirteen), are principally trained as architects but are applying their architectural knowledge to graphic design and the production of video graphics using advanced digital editing programs and special-effects software. So the distinctive positions of architecture and graphics are becoming increasingly blurred. The use of computer programs allows practices to move out of the parameters of their design discipline. Each of the firms featured in this book who work solely in the digital medium are careful to emphasize that, although computers are integral tools in the design process, the projects are generated from a strong conceptual basis.

Marshall McLuhan's well worn quote, "the medium is the message," is hotly denied. When asked what programs Softroom, the multi-media practice from London, uses for its stylized futuristic visions of twenty-first century living for the lifestyle magazine *Wallpaper*, Oliver Salway replied, "People are often surprised that we do not use more cutting-edge programs. To repeat a cliche, "It's not what you have, it's how you use it."

To decipher the relationship between sign (the graphics) and form (the architecture) it is interesting to look at exhibition graphics, where the integration of graphic design and three-dimensional design has progressed dramatically. As audiences become increasingly more exposed to sophisticated computer animations (and the interpretation of imagery), the field of exhibition design has had to keep pace. The traditional method of object/caption is viewed as didactic and unappealing. At the same time exhibition design should not be too overpowering and subordinate the displayed objects. In the case of Met Studio's project work for the Digital Gallery, at the National Museum of Photography, Film and Television (see Chapter Six) the integration of the graphics with the execution of the space resulted in the graphics

and text panels becoming representations of three-dimensional space. The graphics were explored as the possible interaction between space and information.

In the field of domestic and retail interiors, 24/seven's design of the hairdresser the Klinik, in London (see Chapter Seven) is not a literal transposition of text but introduces an architectural vocabulary that denotes an evocation of atmosphere through surface, materials, and composition. The application of graphics as an informative communication tool is not a feature. The clinical atmosphere of the Klinik is reflected in the sterility of the space with the display of white leather furnishings and cool blue lighting. Regarding the translation of graphic design theory being applied to architecture, Softroom's graphic style of simulated hyper-real surfaces (Chapter Eleven) appears to seamlessly transcribe to the design of the architectural pavilion. The pavilion's external skin mirrors and distorts the surrounding landscape, invoking a subtle degree of artifice.

PRINCIPAL	TONKIN: MIKE TONKIN	LOCATION	TONKIN: HONG KONG, LONDON	YEAR FOUNDED	TONKIN: 1998
	HYBRID: DAVID BOTHWELL ALICE LEE		HYBRID: HONG KONG, LONDON		HYBRID: 1995

With the levelling out of hierarchies in design, graphic designers are being invited to apply their ideas to three-dimensional space. Aptly suited to such a task, graphic designers can react spontaneously to cultural shifts, perfectly suited to the design of bars, clubs, and retail outlets whose interiors have to respond to contemporary cultural ideas.

Tonkin Architects has collaborated with graphic designers on a number of projects. With offices in Hong Kong and now London, the firm completed a stream of bars and clubs with very strong graphic influences. In its design of three Hong Kong projects, graphic design firm Hybrid worked alongside Tonkin Architects as full members of the design team, from the initial stages of the project through to the construction phase. Hybrid sees its role not as an add-on to Tonkin's skills but as a process of bringing graphic design skills to the team.

Tonkin's recent monograph, *asking, looking, playing, making,* describes its approach to design in a visual treatise that underlines its approach to creating its own very distinctive design identity. This is where Hybrid enters the picture. Each of the three projects selected demonstrate a bias to theming the design to match the client's ethos, which could be the identity of the bar, or in the case of the Broadway cinemas, the branding of the cinema chain. Often clients would require design services from the interior space right down to the company's business card. Hybrid's strong, almost contemporary constructivist vocabulary incorporated bold geometrical forms. Tonkin approached Hybrid, graphic designers, also based in Hong Kong, to collaborate on the illustrated projects.

The four selected projects—a bar, Flex; a karaoke bar/nightclub, Tong Zhi, and two cinemas from the Broadway chain—all testify to Hong Kong's high life. In the case of the cinemas, Hybrid was asked to create a retail identity for a new chain of cinemas in Hong Kong. Tonkin approached Hybrid explaining their concept of the "spectacle" for the cinema chain. Thus red, the color of blood, was chosen as the pivotal design reference because of its association with the theatre and bullring connotations.

Although the design team has a very strong visual identity, it describes its methodology of working as searching for developing concepts that are specific to person, place, and time. The goal being "to originate concepts that will stay true and be understood through archetypal forms." The design philosophy is to produce architecture that is both particular and accessible.

Tonkin's commitment to searching out the truly contemporary in direct defiance to modernist doctrine is spelled out in the following quote: "The best details are the ones that disappear. The whole is more important than the parts. Intensify by reduction and expand with illusion." The application of illusion is played out in the close collaboration with the graphic designers. This is best illustrated in the Flex bar with a disorientating labyrinth of passages creating the impression of depth that far outdoes the slim dimensions of the site.

Tong Zhi Karaoke Bar

CLIENT TONG ZHI

PROJECT DESCRIPTION KARAOKE BAR IDENTITY AND INTERIOR DESIGN—HONG KONG

DATE 1996

2

3

tóng zhì

1 The red, yellow, and cream interlocking pattern on a dark brown background was inspired by a wallpaper pattern book from the 1970s full of wacky, psychedelic designs. "The wallpaper design is similar to Chinese calligraphy but is also reminiscent of a 1970s Prada pattern and a bit like a jungle," says Mike Tonkin.

2 The business card designed for Joe Cheng, the director of Tóng Zhì, uses the crisp, almost hieroglyphic design of the wallpaper pattern.

3 Soft white sofas and bar stools echo the shape of the wallpaper motif but keep a low profile in the space.

When Tonkin Architects was commissioned to design a karaoke bar/nightclub, the practice delved into a catalog full of 1970s wallpaper patterns. Consequently, the central motif of this project is the repeated interlocking pattern of red, yellow, and cream on a dark-brown background—a graphic that appears in the club's interior design, logo, and business card. The design was inspired by the wacky, psychedelic forms taken from a wallpaper pattern book that was found in a derelict building in Hong Kong. "It is similar to Chinese calligraphy but is also reminiscent of a 1970s Prada pattern and a bit like a jungle," says Mike Tonkin. Soft white-glass and bar stools on stalks (manufactured in

China to keep the project to a very low budget) echo but do not compete with the shapes of the red, yellow, and cream motif.

The interlocking pattern was also inspired by the soft angles of a computer-generated image of the nightclub's floor plan. To execute the pattern, it was more economical to manufacture a galvanized steel stencil than a one-off wallpaper. The pattern was then drawn onto the wall and painted. The design of the business card for Joe Cheng, the owner of Tóng Zhì, uses the crisp, almost hieroglyphic design of the wallpaper pattern.

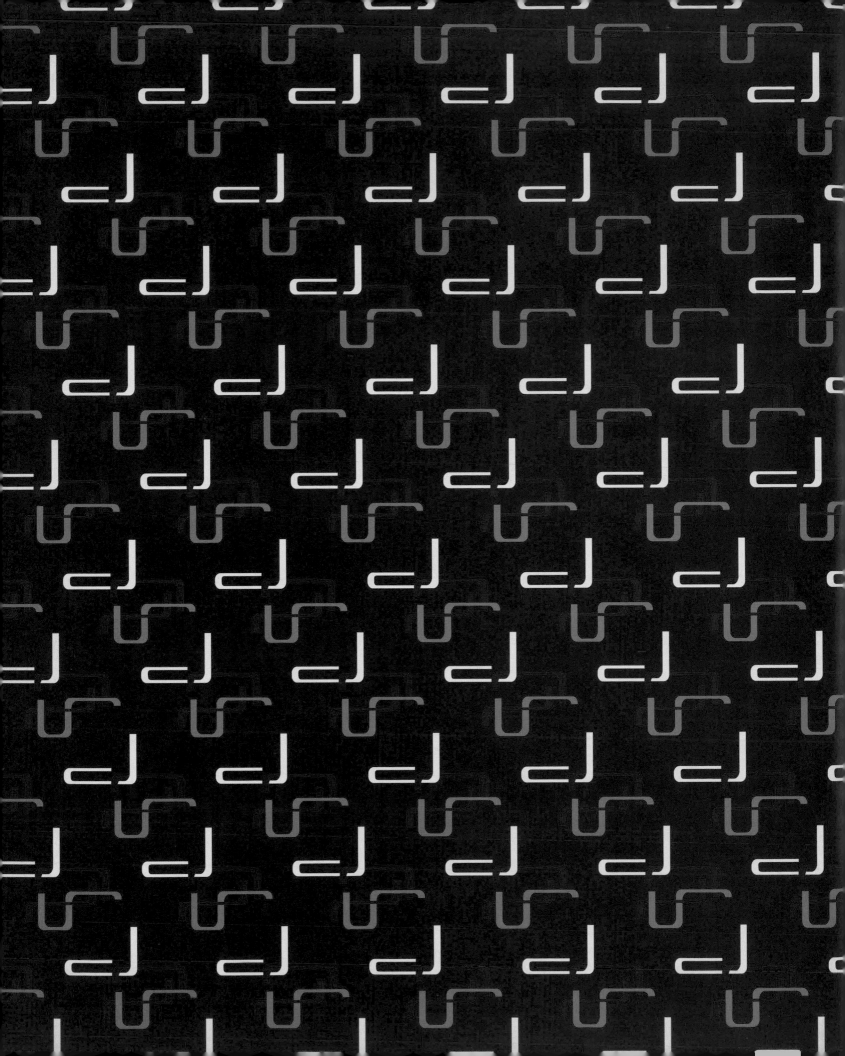

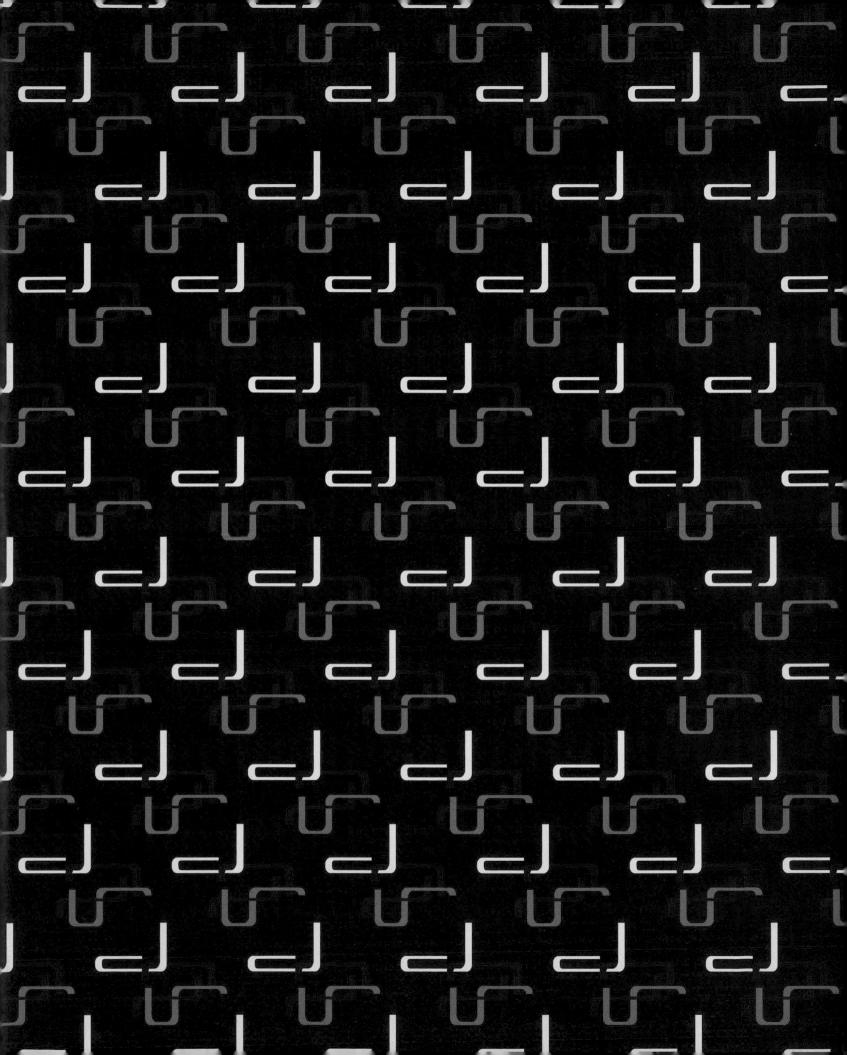

CLIENT

PROJECT DESCRIPTION

DATE

Yuen Long Cinema

BROADWAY CINEMAS

CINEMA IDENTITY AND LOBBY DESIGN—HONG KONG

1996

1 The foyer area, which features a processional route up to the screens, has a blown up image of Roger Moore wallpapered onto the wall.

2 Projected light forms the bases for the cinematic moving image.

3 Yuen Long was the first of a new chain of cinemas in Hong Kong, for which Hybrid was asked to create a retail identity.

4 The cinema's new logo, a lower case "b" in a circle, was projected around the cinema.

5 The plan and section illustrate the extent of the red hue that was used as a blank canvas for the foyer and circulation areas.

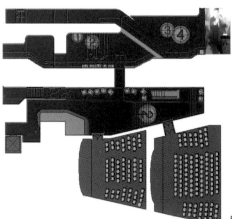

5

Tonkin Architects collaborated with Hybrid on a series of Hong Kong cinemas that are saturated with film iconography, where huge countdown numbers taken from early film reels are projected obliquely across the space, blurring the distinction between floor, walls, and ceiling. Hybrid was asked to create a retail identity for this new chain of cinemas, called Broadway; Tonkin Architects approached Hybrid with the concept of the "spectacle" for the cinema chain. Thus red, the color of blood, was selected as the pivotal design reference because of its strong theatrical associations and bull-ring connotations. The plan and section of Yuen Long, the first of these cinemas, illustrate the extent to which the color red was used as a "blank canvas" for the foyer and circulation areas.

Large numbers, projected throughout the lobby and enlarged to a diameter of approximately 13 feet (4 meters), represent the countdown at the beginning of a film and also indicate the number of screens within each cinema house. Ceiling lights, designed by Tonkin, hang down forming islands of light in the main foyer areas. The cinema's new logo, a lower case "b" in a circle, is also projected around the cinema. The foyer area, which displays a processional route up to the screens, has a blown up image of Roger Moore wallpapered onto the 39.5 foot by 16.5 foot (12 meters by 5 meters) wall.

Mong Kok Cinema

CLIENT **BROADWAY CINEMA**

PROJECT DESCRIPTION **CINEMA IDENTITY AND LOBBY DESIGN–HONG KONG**

DATE **1996**

1

CLIENT
PROJECT DESCRIPTION
DATE

Flex Bar
JETT INVESTORS
INTERIOR DESIGN—HONG KONG
1996

3

4

1 and 3 Stalactite-like forms
are suspended from the ceiling, which house video monitors showing kitsch films.
Light was the key concept
that Hybrid worked with,
resulting in light coming
solely from the video
screens or projected beams.

4 The passage is contructed
of secondary walls with projected beams of light. The
aim is sensory disorienta-
tion, as men move through
the mauve passage.

2 The simple and functional
door detail demonstrates
Tonkin's expression of architecture that is more about
creating a dramatic atmosphere than a concern with
the minutiae of detailing.

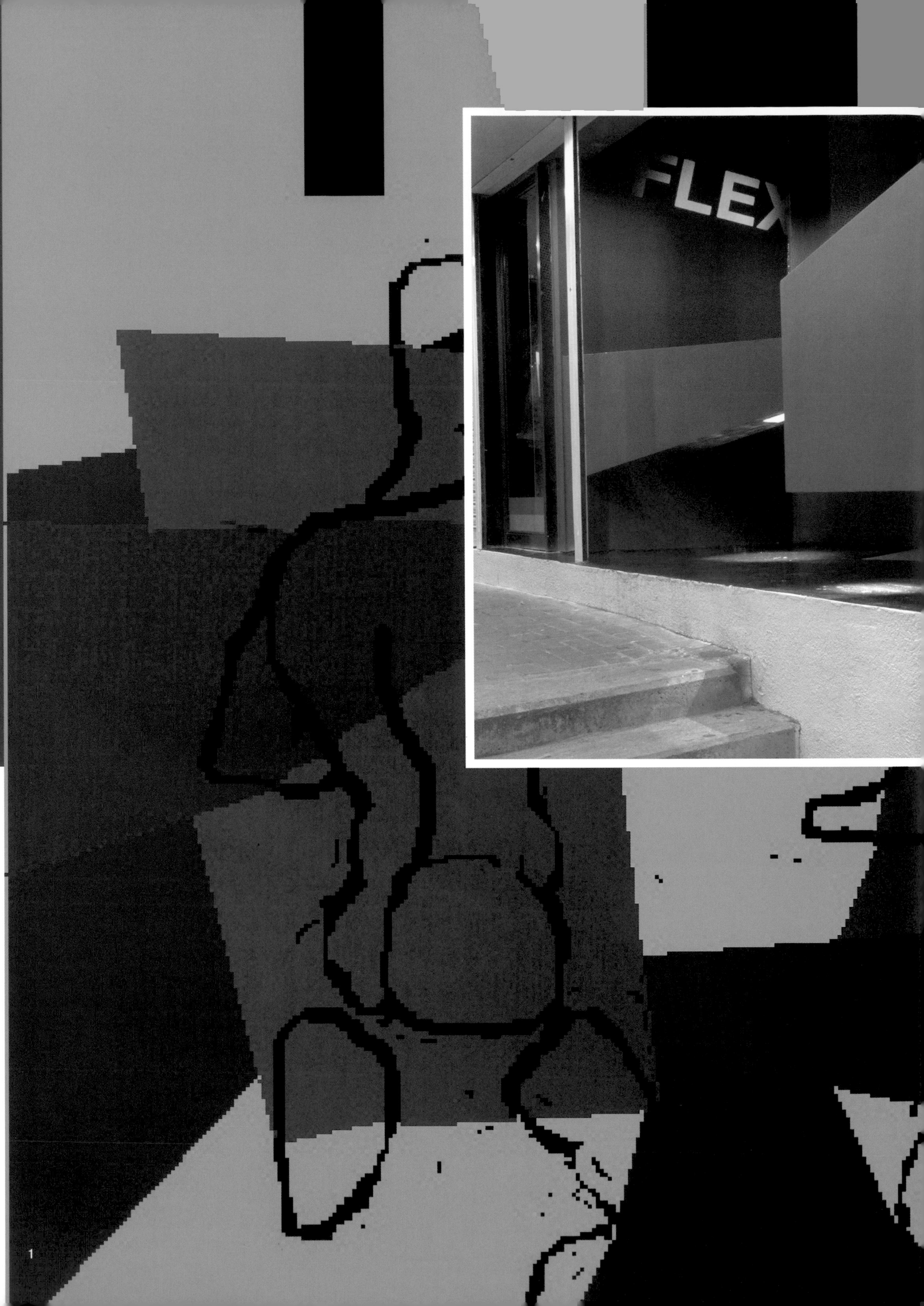

1

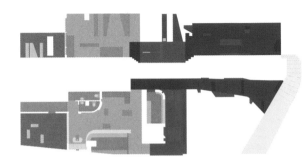

FLEX 7 GLENEALY RD CENTRAL HK
中環己連拿利道7號 2526 4328

2   3   4

1 A mural, designed by
Hybrid, was placed on the
wall in the bar area featuring
abstracted male forms,
which acts as a
reflection/backdrop to the
dance floor and further distorts the visitor's experience
of scale and space.

2 and 3 It was decided that
a conventional logo for Flex
was unnecessary and that
the graphics should be
almost invisible. Therefore,
the interior space had no lettering, while the exterior had
the name Flex projected
onto the wall, only while the
bar was open.

4 The plan led the clients
through a maze of forms and
light, providing a combination of intimate spaces and
open areas.

Ben Kelly Design Studio with Lippa Pearce and Associated Images

	PRINCIPAL	BK: BEN KELLY	LOCATION	BK: LONDON	YEAR FOUNDED	BEN KELLY: 1977
	PRINCIPAL	LP: HARRY PEARCE, DOMENIC LIPPA, GILES CALVER		LP: TWICKENHAM AI: LONDON		LIPPA PEARCE: 1990 ASSORTED IMAGES: 1990
	ARTIST	AI: TIM HEAD/CHARLIE HOOK				

Ben Kelly's work delights in the everyday quality of design. He has an ability to appropriate design conventions and translate them into innovative and eyecatching applications. From out of Britain's notorious street culture of the 80's came a loose anti-establishment movement that was reflected in fashion, music, and design, best exemplified by the fashion duo Vivienne Westwood and Malcolm McLaren.

The couple, who dressed such notorious bands as The Sex Pistols, turned to Ben Kelly in 1977 to design their legendary shop Seditionaries on London's King's Road. The shop front with steel grates and a bare fluorescent strip lights signified the desired rugged aesthetic style of ghettoised chic.

This theme was to continue, most notably in the design of the seminal nightclub, the Hacienda, situated in the heart of north England's clubland, Manchester, a project which established Kelly's distinctive style. Kelly was appointed as designer of the club with the help of Peter Saville, graphic designer with whom Kelly collaborated. First, the duo worked on a number of highly influential album covers for bands such as Roxy Music and New Order, which have spurred many imitations. The latest joint project to date is a bachelor pad in the heart of London's chic Mayfair penthouse district.

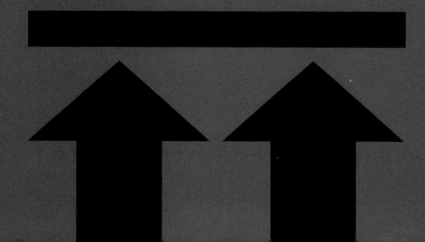

Halfords Stores

HALFORDS
HALFORDS AUTO DEPOT-SHEFIELD AND SWANSEA-ENGLAND
AUGUST 1999

INSTALLATION OF:
ICE
ALARMS
WHEEL & TYRE
COMBINATIONS
TYRES
SUSPENSION
EXHAUSTS

4

5

25 WORKSHOP TOOLS

24 WORKSHOP TOOLS

TOOL BOXES
STORAGE
SOCKET SETS
TOOLS
HANDTOOLS
POWER TOOLS
POWER TOOL ACCESSORIES
AIR COMPRESSORS

1 The vivid strips that refer to road markings take on a literal significance, directing the customer round the store and, at the same time, providing a powerful complement to the tough industrial look.

2 The floor is used as a surface to communicate directional and retail information.

3 The oversized chevrons painted onto the automated Fitting Bay windows provide a dramatic play on scale, adding to the inversion of the traditional shed structure.

4 The fitting bay takes on the language of American-style service stations. Bold vinyl lettering advertises the services offered.

5 Robust materials used to construct the sheds include Douglas fir, galvanized steel, zinc passivated wire mesh, telegraph poles, industrial floor finishes, Western Red Cedar, and industrial strip lighting.

Halfords, Europe's biggest retailer of motor parts commissioned Ben Kelly Design Studio (BKD) to work with Lippa Pearce Design to create a new warehouse concept for its accessories store. The impressive result was an integration of graphic design and architecture from concept stage to finished design. The design elements delved into the vocabulary of road iconography selecting oversized chevrons and arrows to direct customers through the aisles.

The Halfords Auto Depot desired a warehouse with a "no frills" feel in order to accommodate a large range of products at low prices for the autos specialist. The adoption of the industrial shed structure combined with the graphic articulation of the main façade is an ingenious solution to a low-cost fast track method of construction. The "fitting bay," which plays an important role within the store, was designed to be

highly visible from both inside and out. A hole was punched into the corrugated steel clad façade that delineates the bay. The bold graphic style fused together the 3-D and 2-D elements of the project.

The signage is an example of the clarity of graphics, which is carried through to every detail of the project, and even becomes integrated with the walls and floors. The graphics permeated both internal and external surfaces; for example, black and yellow chevrons are painted onto the side of the galvanized corrugated steel façade cladding. The existing shelving system was customized to produce a new hybrid system, which became the heart of the scheme complete with designed corner guards that add to the colorful floorscape.

The applied paint finishes were highly polished, giving the sense of a clinical and clean operational area.

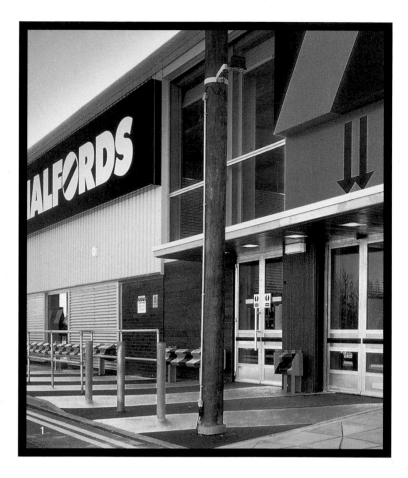

1

CLIENT
PROJECT DESCRIPTION
DATE

Children's Gallery

NATIONAL MUSEUM OF SCIENCE AND INDUSTRY
MUSEUM GALLERY
FEBRUARY 1995

2

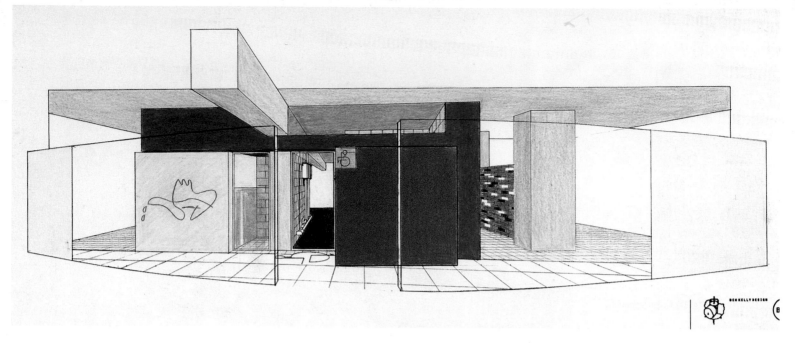

3

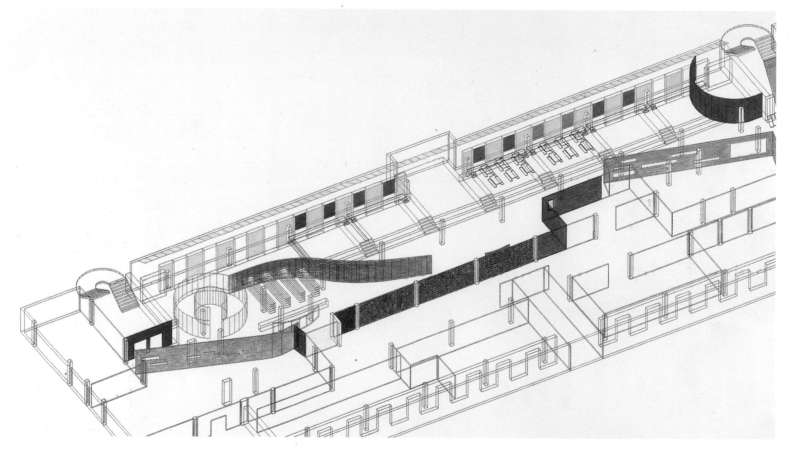

1 Information panels are set off against Kelly's trademark of using road marking language, in this case chevrons painted directly onto the concrete. Assorted Images has turned the shop signage 'eat drink shop' into a sculptural object.

2 The proposal for a bold and colorful intervention is in stark contrast to the existing concrete structure.

3 The axonometric shows the existing basement with the overlaying terraces. The colored walls depict the separation between the open area and the designated education rooms such as The Garden, Things, and The Secret Life of the Home, each of which was designed by independent interior design firms.

This was the first collaborative project between Assorted Images and BKD. Based in the heart of Soho, London's film industry ghetto, Assorted Images extends beyond the printed text having designed the latest British Broadcasting Companies prestigious Design Awards Exhibition and video graphics. The two firms were brought together when London's major museum dedicated to Science and Industry underwent a complete internal modernization.

the terrac

the terrace

1 The basement's original structure of 600 mm (2 ft) steel I-beams bolted to columns was reinforced in the 1980s with cast in-situ concrete. The concrete structure has been removed in parts to reveal the original beam, which is painted with intumescent paint.

2 The central bay of the ceiling in the multifunctional space has been painted in reflective paint and diffusion panels have been suspended in front of a track of lighting to create the impression of natural light flooding into the space.

3 The dimpled surface of the glass brick walls provides a degree of opacity to the toilets. The galvanized steel duct channels are designed to reinforce the symmetry of the existing structure.

4 (next page) A gentle ramp wrapped by a wall constructed of glazed bricks brings the children into the basement gallery. In the foreground is an example of artist Tim Head's waste objects—the plastic bottle ring head that secures a disposable bottle head.

The existing children's area was deemed to be dull and unappealing rather than visually stimulating to animate the children's senses. The multifunctional space needed to accommodate up to 2,500 school children a day. The solution incorporates a series of terraces and provides a shop, toilets, and three galleries.

To do this BKD designed the overall masterplan of the area. One of the objectives behind the design brief was that the basement gallery provides an educational resource in a playful way. This is demonstrated in the articulation of the construction of structural elements; i.e. the exposure of the electrical circuits and stripping down of the cladding materials to reveal the column and beam structure. In addition, the curator selected a number of artists to apply their work to the space. Among them was Tim Head, a sculptor by training. Head sifted through what he termed as twentieth-century consumer waste—bubble packaging for tablets, ring pull cans and disposable cutlery. The objects were photographed, enlarged and then incorporated into the linoleum floors of the main concourse. Another example of the selected artwork is Charlie Hooke's "indoor lightning," a gold-leaf covered, metal box built into one of the basement walls. Activated by visitors, the devise sends out a 70,000-volt electric spark that creates lightning bolts.

the garden

for 3 to 6s

1

2

3

the garden

for 3 to 6

4

1 Graphic panels are made of photo symbols of children and objects, photographed informally and integrated within the vitreous enamel signage system. Sassoon typeface was used based on readability research for the target audience of three- to seventeen-year olds.

2 The entrance to the children's gallery is situated in the museum's underbelly. The term 'environmental graphics' describes the way-finding signage that wraps around the gallery's entrance.

3 The graphics and architecture are unified to create the impression of airport arrival and departure terminals. The heating and electrical services are highlighted in bright colors or by articulating them in galvanized aluminium encasements.

4 Ben Kelly's abstraction of the dividing wall to the garden is complemented by the layering of the graphic panels. The garden gallery is an interpretation of an urban garden, translated into a play space with a wet area incorporating machinery that teases, dams and flows water through nozzles, spouts, and shoots.

PRINCIPAL | ROSS HUNTER | LOCATION | GLASGOW | YEAR FOUNDED | 1986
JANICE KIRKPATRICK

Design duo Ross Hunter and Janice Kirkpatrick established
Graven Images in 1986. The two trained in different disciplines:
Hunter as an architect and Kirkpatrick as a graphic designer. The
practice was founded on the European cross-disciplinary model.
"We were influenced by movements that were evolving in the '80s,
such as Memphis, where there was no clear delineation between
professions," says Hunter. Memphis, the avant-garde design group
from Milan was led by Ettore Sottsass and consisted of designers
from a variety of disciplines, intent on offering a radical alternative
to minimalist tenets and exploring issues of popular taste.

Graven Images does not have a policy of divisionalism in the office; commissions are spread across the board. Hunter feels that the idea of departmentalizing design is a retrogressive step stemming from the system of British design education, which breeds separatism rather than fostering an environment of communication.

Each designer brings different qualities to a project, but both are unified in their desire to bolster Glasgow's international standing. Graven Images is now considered one of the leading design houses in Scotland and is expanding far beyond its immediate geographical surroundings with commissions in London's Millennium Dome and international touring exhibitions. "It was a conscious decision to be in Glasgow," Hunter explains. "It was a mission to prove it was possible to do the kind of work we wanted to do from here. Work not just with a local importance, but with an international relevance." For Kirkpatrick, it's the city's inhabitants that make the crucial difference.

Graven Image's body of work spans a broad spectrum of projects. Commissioned by Glasgow City Council to design its logo, the result was a sensitive blending of green, white, and orange in a city more associated with varying hues of gray. The logo is an ubiquitous element that adorns the city, appearing on council vehicles, school signs, and city information signage. During the early years, the practice took on a broad mixture of work, such as flyers and posters for Glasgow's underground culture. The company now employs a staff of approximately seventeen people, and invites other professionals, such as artists, musicians, and academics, to collaborate on projects when appropriate.

The practice takes a holistic approach to design. In all three of the selected projects, the graphics and interior design is combined seamlessly, enabling the identity of the client to be subtly recognized without being interpreted as obvious branding.

CLIENT
PROJECT DESCRIPTION
DATE

RATT
MR & MRS WILLIAM FERGUSON
SCOTLAND NIGHT CLUB
DECEMBER 1997

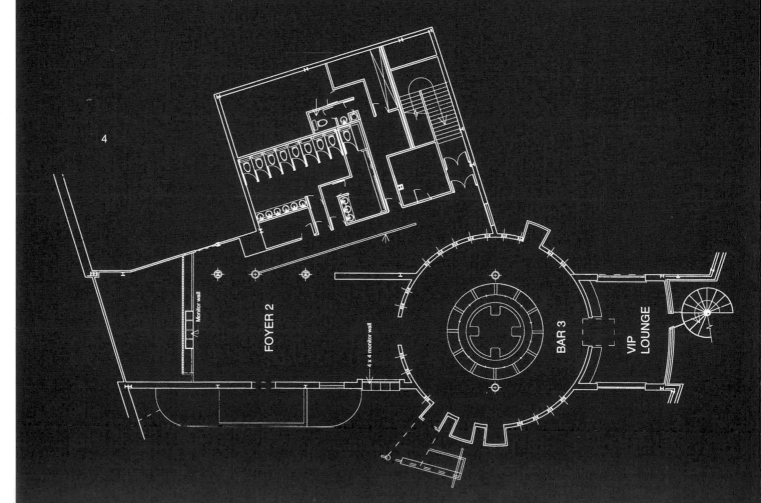

1

4

FOYER 2

Monitor wall

4 x 4 monitor wall

BAR 3

VIP
LOUNGE

2

3

1 The club in live action complete with gobo lighting and strobescopic effects.

2 Graven Images uses the recurring motif of a large image placed within a circle, in this case the star.

3 The night club's logo, designed by Graven Images, is an abstraction of the letter 'r'. The logo has been purposely abstracted to resemble a symbol rather than a letter.

4 & 5 The circular bar is the pivotal form around which the plan is designed.

next page

1 The RATT logo set off against a light sculpture using fluorescent light strips. The sculpture is inspired by the work of the fluorescent light sculptor Dan Flavin.

2 Live action at the RATT.

A nightclub with 1,500 square meters of floor space, Room at the Top (RATT) was designed to house three dance floors, three bars, a VIP suite and a bistro to accommodate up to 2,500 people. The client purchased an industrial shed with a trussed roof into which Graven Images inserted a hierarchy of forms. The plan is shaped like a shuttlecock, with a circular bar acting as the pivotal feature. The interior design scheme takes advantage of exposed structural elements as well as dramatic color schemes.

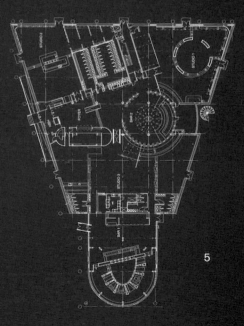

5

1

2

5

6

3

4

7

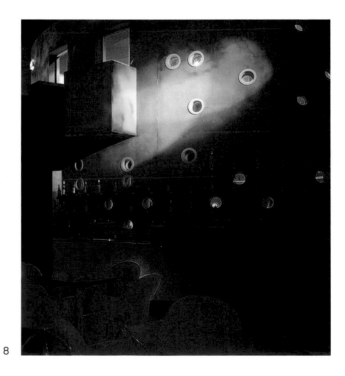

8

1 A section of toughened glass cut to a radii links intimate spaces to overall views.

2 The vibrant and bright color scheme of the ground floor recalls the soft shades of the '50s, while the more subdued and evocative musty colors of the upper floors is reminiscent of American speakeasies.

3 The existing structure of trusses and corrugated aluminum was left exposed. Graven Images used low-cost materials in imaginative ways, such as varying wooden veneers on the table and bench tops.

4 The DJ's booth is supported on a mild steel column which sits on a mild steel I-beam, with metal decking and plywood as the floor covering. Concrete slabs hold the decks providing a solid base for the turntables.

5 The floor was treated like a blank canvas on which Graven Images arranged Dalsouple rubber floor tiles in an abstracted pattern to complement the furniture and wall coverings.

6 Bar stools constructed of leather, plywood, and brushed aluminum are anchored to the circular wall of the bar.

7 At night, the gobo lighting and stroboscopic effects permeate the nightclub's interior.

8 View onto the main dance floor with go-go chairs made of polypropylene and cast-aluminum legs.

CLIENT ESCABAR GROUP
PROJECT DESCRIPTION A RESTAURANT IN GLASGOW'S CITY CENTRE
DATE JANUARY 1999

Tun Ton

1

vinyl bands

gold mosiac.

dome

vinyl on glass.

veneer.

light

white jelly

polycarbonate backlit.

fibre optics

led up photo

Adjustable table lights

olive.

mirror

opus romano

bute fabrics

2

EATING.

limestone floor.

1-2 These images illustrate the restaurant layout within the building that originally functioned as a retail store. Graven Images restored the nineteenth century shopfront and retained the original terrazzo flooring in the foyer area. The mezzanine floor plan shows the new stair-case that skirts along the party wall. A glass screen acts as balustrating, which provides a degree of dynamism to the space.

3 The sketch shows the pro-posal for the introduction of a mezzanine floor that increased the potential of the high ceilings without compromising the airiness of the space.

Driven by an awareness of what is lacking in the city—and a desire to fill the gaping void of entertainment—Graven Image's most recent project Tun Ton adds a suave and elegant restaurant/bar to Glasgow's choice of nightlife venues. Situated in the heart of Glasgow's city center, Tun Ton is ideally placed to attract business people during the day and a fashion-conscious crowd in the evenings. A rapidly expanding leisure group

in Scotland named Escobar commissioned Graven Images to design Tun Ton in a Victorian building with grand windows at the ground floor level. Graven Images restored the original windows that had been previously covered up to allow natural day light to flow freely into the space. An elegant staircase was inserted, which leads to a mezzanine level.

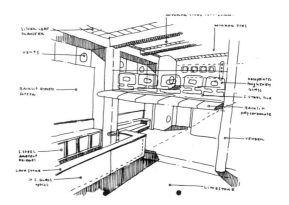

1

pages 50-53

An elegant staircase leads up to the mezzanine floor. The treads, clad in white rubber Dalsoupe, are supported on a continuous steel stringer. The columns are clad in Bisazza Glass Mosaic tiles.

CLIENT
PROJECT DESCRIPTION
DATE

Favorit

MONTPELIER
DELECATESSEN AND BAR
JUNE 1999

1

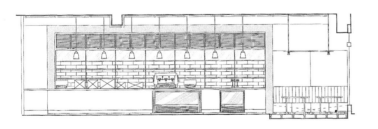

2

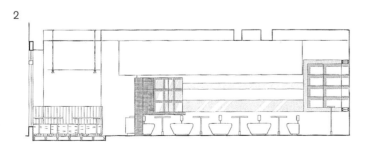

3

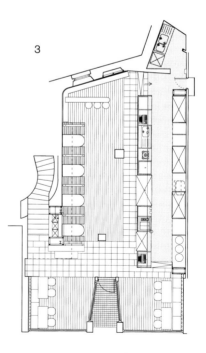

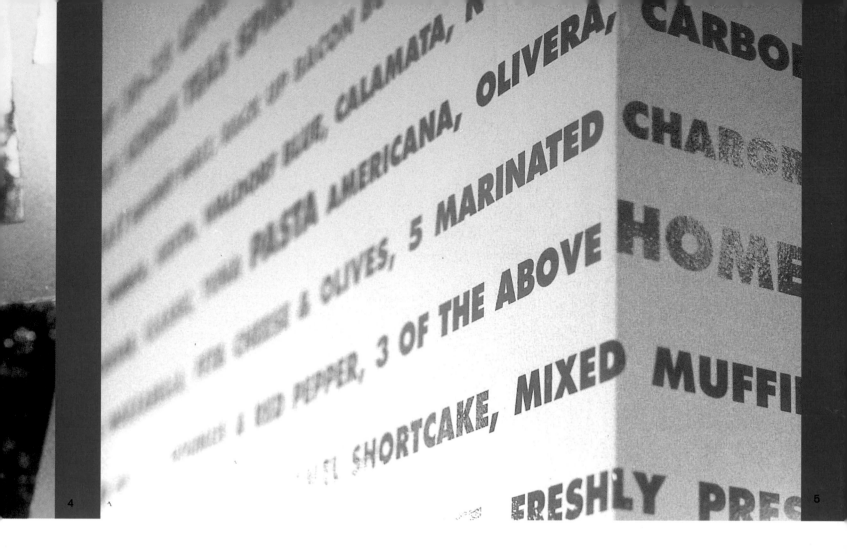

1 The section illustrates the efficient use of shelving that runs the whole length of the serving counter.

2 The section shows the dual seating benches that resemble those normally found in an American diner.

3 An overhead view.

4 The brand Favorit was developed as an entity with the commission encompassing all the graphic elements, print, and signage. This can be clearly seen on the exterior windows, where a stylized type is used to advertise the location.

5 An example of the graphics being used for dual effect—one to communicate what is on the menu; the other text as wallpaper.

next page

1 The designers stressed that they did not want to create a retro look but intended to produce a simple set of elements that could be reproduced, as Favorit would become part of a chain of similar bars. The shelving system is designed to be modular and easily adaptable to each new site. Shelves are stacked with lava lamps, espresso china and Alessi coffee machines.

2 Leather and suede banquettes and chrome booths are reminiscent of the 1950s milk bar style. Favorit has been dubbed a 'fusion bar.'

At Favorit, the loosely termed "bar" is a fusion of a bar, deli, café, and mini-grocery store that offers soft drinks and alcohol from 8 AM to 3 AM. The operational brief given to Graven Images was to create a flexible concept that would suit non-high street, neighborhood locations. For the design, Graven Images redefined some of the classical elements found in traditional Italian cafes—and used robust and timeless materials, such as leather, glass shelving and Formica table tops edged with stainless steel.

1 Zebrano veneer is used as a wall covering to create a warm feeling in the booths. The self-service tear off menu is attached to a stainless steel sheet. Cast-iron radiators reinforce the atmosphere of permanence in the bar.

FAT (Fashion, Architecture and Taste)

PRINCIPAL	SEAN GRIFFITHS	LOCATION	LONDON	YEAR FOUNDED	1993
	SAM JACOB				
	CHARLES HOLLAND				

FAT—an acronym for Fashion, Architecture and Taste—describes itself as an interdisciplinary group of architects, artists, graphic designers and provocateurs seeking to enliven contemporary cultural production through the cross-fertilization of ideas and processes. FAT's projects have ranged from the design of night-clubs and domestic interiors to the curation of exhibits in non-gallery contexts, such as bus shelters, shopping bags, and billboards.

FAT's ambitious manifesto aims to explode the container of the art gallery and blur the boundaries of fine art and architecture in the built environment. The practice has adopted a populist design vocabulary that introduces elements of domestic kitsch and leisure culture. The premise aims to expose the myth of modernism as an outmoded theory that has been reduced from its doctrinal manifesto to a mere stylistic vocabulary.

The design of the Kesselskramer offices in Amsterdam culminated in a fusion of ideas between FAT and the client, a Dutch advertising agency renowned for its paradigm-breaking work methods. The two partners—Eric Kessels and Joahn Kramer—and their small staff are known for positivism, humor, and disregard for glossing over the truth. Labeled as "anti-advertising guerrillas," the agency has been cutting a fine line between what is deemed acceptable and what is offensive in advertisement standards. Recent campaigns have featured bloody severed

heads for a hairdressing company and to exaggerate a budget hotel's drawbacks, its advertising copy read: "now a door in every room."

Needing larger office space, the agency moved into a nineteenth-century church in central Amsterdam. Listed as a national monument and adorned with original stained glass windows, wooden roof, and steel columns, the building's interior could not be physically altered.

The project did not follow the conventional path of commissioning, approval of scaled working drawings, schedule of works and final site supervision. Instead, both practices—known for breaking out of the parameters of conventional professional relationships—applied their own idiosyncratic methodology of work. FAT offered Kesselskramer a catalogue of architectural furniture from which to choose. The selection included boats, jetties, goal posts, a Russian

fort, a "Baywatch" beach tower, areas of a football pitch, and an over-scaled garden shed. This combination of popular cultural icons, combined with the agency's own idiosyncratic collection of objects, created a tongue-in-cheek dialogue set against the ecclesiastical context. In the process, the interior of the church remained untouched.

Although the architectural typology was selected in a playful way, the haphazardness of the floor plan belies a careful architectonic plan and zoning of functions. Kesselskramer is delighted with the space, which can be easily deconstructed, packed up, and reinstalled. FAT's design, which applies graphic iconography to a three-dimensional space—invests a vocabulary that combines performance and imagery. The space is the antithesis to the orthodox, minimalist office space, and reinvents architecture's relationship to its user.

CLIENT
PROJECT DESCRIPTION
DATE

Kesselskramer

KESSELSKRAMER-AMSTERDAM
ADVERTISING OFFICE
JULY 1999

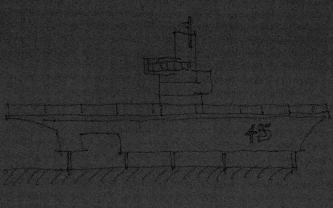

PIER   AIRCRAFT CARRIER

2

3

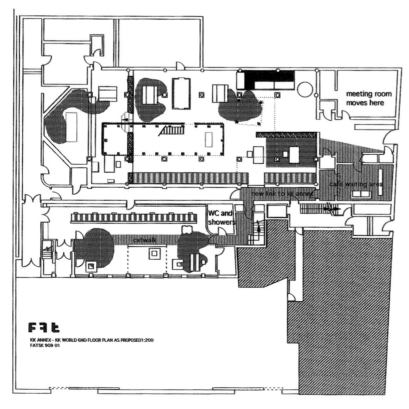

meeting room moves here

café waiting area

new link to KK annex

WC and showers

catwalk

FAT

KK ANNEX - KK WORLD GND FLOOR PLAN AS PROPOSED 1:200
FATSK 909 01

1 (previous page) The photograph shows the main built interventions. All departments within the agency have their own spaces and there are generous common areas. The intention was to blur the boundaries between client and employee.

2 The sketches illustrate some of the architectural and graphic icons from which Kesselskramer made its selections.

3 The plan shows the insertion of objects placed within the existing church structure. The office's catwalk reinforces the linear entrance through the refectory and accentuates one's arrival into the main office area. The church is virtually untouched by FAT's design.

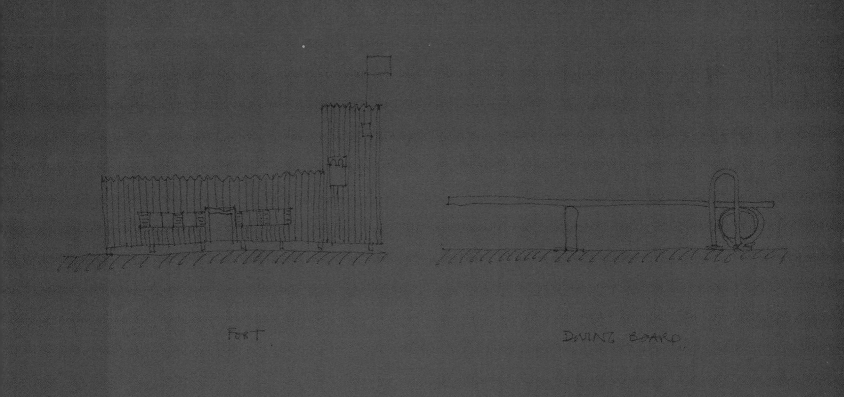

FORT   DIVING BOARD

68/69

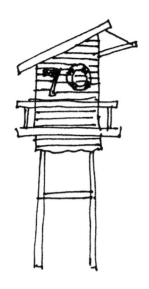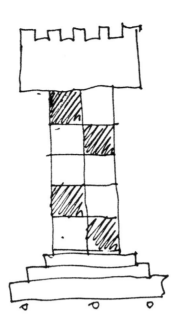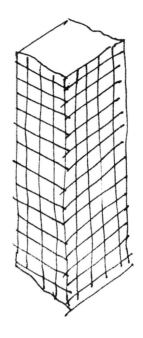

LIFEGUARD TOWER.　　　SEIGE TOWER.　　　MINIATURE SKYSCRAPER.

previous page No obvious
company logo was intro-
duced into the overall
design; instead FAT's desig-
nation of areas is annotated
using the playful language of
leisure. Where text may have
been introduced, graphics
are substituted by emblems,
such as the recycled, tubular
fluorescent OPEN shop sign
or the life-saving ring.

PRINCIPAL	14 PRINCIPALS	LOCATION	PG: LONDON, NY, AUSTIN, SAN FRAN	YEAR FOUNDED	PG: 1972
	RMO: BOBBY OAKLEY		RMO: USA		
	ALLIANCE: JAMES SNOW		ALLIANCE: USA		

Founded in 1972, the design consultancy Pentagram is unusual in its structure—a multidisciplinary firm made up of a confederation of small teams lead by partners from different disciplines. It undertakes projects ranging from brochures to collaborations on built projects.

Pentagram's designs—from Kenneth Grange's Kodak "Instamatic" to the styling of the British 125 train—have been granted the status of seminal objects, and, in turn, summarize the importance of design's role in society as "a serious instrument for communicating culture in the contemporary world."

Pentagram constantly re-appraises its position and re-invents itself in response to trends in visual communications. The ability to embrace art, design, and commerce without one element being subsumed by another means that designs have an air of longevity, such as the "Venner" parking meter, designed in 1983 and still in use to this day.

The company has remained independent from the influence of Modernism. It embraces the view that graphics is about pluralism without slipping into eclecticism. The key word is communication.

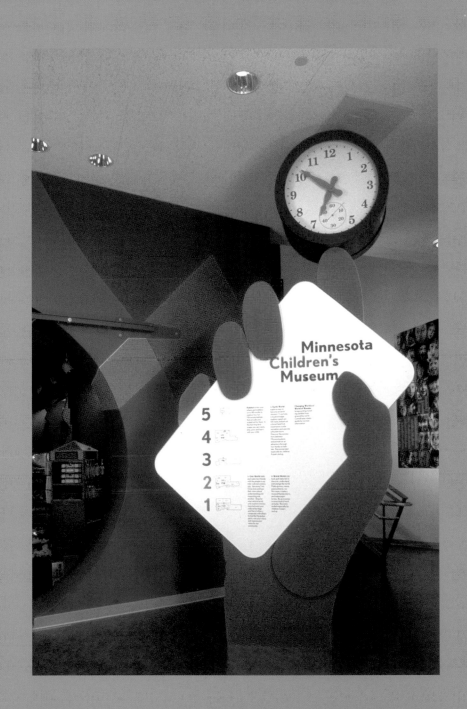

CLIENT
PROJECT DESCRIPTION
DATE

MINNESOTA CHILDREN'S MUSEUM
GRAPHIC PROGRAM
1995

Minnesota Children's Museum

3

1 The hand theme was introduced as indicators for the museum's floor levels and room number signs. Raised fingers, counting from one to five, mark the floor levels.

2 The girl's bathroom sign, pictured here, takes on the symbol used universally to indicate the female sex. The use of a child's hand to demonstrate the sign adds a degree of humor.

3 The hand and ball motif creates a powerful link between the museum program and its physical presence and establishes a place for children to return to.

4 (next page) In the final frame of the temporary photo mural, Pentagram replaced the red ball with one of the museum's porthole windows, reinforcing the strong relationship between the graphic design program and the architecture of the museum.

Pentagram, with architects James/Snow and The Alliance, responded quite literally to the Minnesota Children's Museum's request to emphasize its reputation for being a hands-on learning center. The design team, lead by Michael Beirut, developed a graphic program based on children's hands photographed in gestures of active exploration. This sign language is meant to appeal to a child's sense of irony and humor using bold colorful photographic work but avoiding cliches, such as the use of crayons or poster paints. The museum appeals to a broad group of children from the ages of five up to fifteen.

The second major feature of the graphic program is the red ball, derived from the architecture of the museum. The ball is applied to windows, doors, and other elements and acts as the subject of the hand's exploration—i.e., the ball is grasped, spun, and miraculously balanced in the photographic signs. The graphic theme was announced in a 40-foot-high photo that temporarily hung in front of the museum.

4

1

2

1 Introducing conventional architectural plans to indicate the building's layout provides clear diagrammatic information. The recurring theme of the red ball in the design appears in three dimensions as the signage's mounting hardware.

2 Graphics articulate the building's features such as these double doors. Vinyl prints were applied to veneered doors.

3 Constructed with MDF, the over-scaled, three-dimensional hand balances a clock. In the background, children enter the shop through a circular entrance cut into the brightly colored walls.

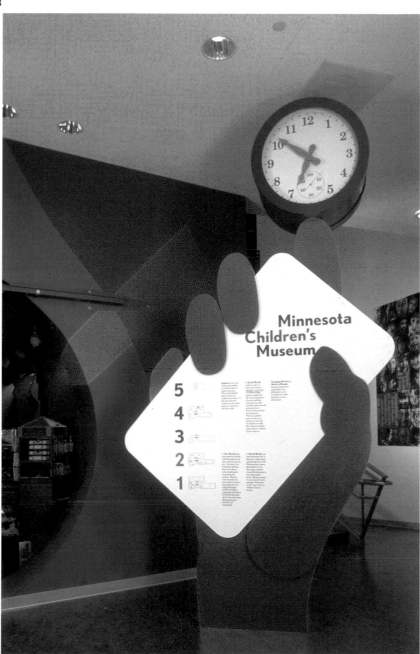

PRINCIPAL | CHRIS CAWTE   LOCATION | LONDON   YEAR FOUNDED | 1982

The multidisciplinary practice Met Studio grew up in '80s Britain, taking its name from its original base, the Metropolitan Wharf in Wapping, London. Met Design has stood the test of time, surviving Britain's boom and bust period, by building up a strong client base from museums in Taiwan to the Virgin Group and Welcome Trust. Awarded amongst stiff competition, the commission to design Britain's first gallery solely dedicated to new digital media provided a challenging opportunity to combine graphic design with exhibition design.

The gallery, Wired Worlds—Exploring the Digital Frontier, is located within the National Museum of Photography, Film and Television in northern England.

The design challenge was to transform a concrete box, which had previously functioned as an art gallery with basic lighting, into an environment that could explore digital technology's application and its implications—and appeal to both the technophobe and technophile. There, an exploration of electronic and conventional imaging and the possibilities of digital technology is balanced against the moral and ethical questions raised by the digital revolution. The original intention was to create the world's first graphic free gallery—to communicate information through an interactive system of information. However, budget restrictions meant that static text had to be introduced.

To convey these messages, the curators and Met Studio commissioned international artists to respond to these issues.

Met's in-house graphic team, described as "typographic nuts," responded to the design concept that embraced an exploration into the fourth dimension of space. The response was to produce normal text panels, distorted as if projected at an angle onto the facing plane. Another design feature to create the illusion of text being suspended in space was introduced with screen-printed text in UV ink on translucent boards. When illuminated the text appears to rise from the surface to produce a three-dimensional effect.

On entering Wired Worlds the visitor is led down a corridor lined with LEDs activated by movement sensors. The sensors send

pulses of different patterns creating an interactive screen. The piece was conceived by the digital artist Nigel Johnson and executed by Met. All the workings of the structure are revealed to engage the visitor with its mechanisms. The overall impression of the gallery is the antithesis to the white box of the computer. Circuit boards, information systems, and computer language spill out in front of the spectator's eyes.

The German artists ART & COM designed a piece that globally tracks e-movement around the world monitoring the day's Internet activities through a satellite map of the globe.

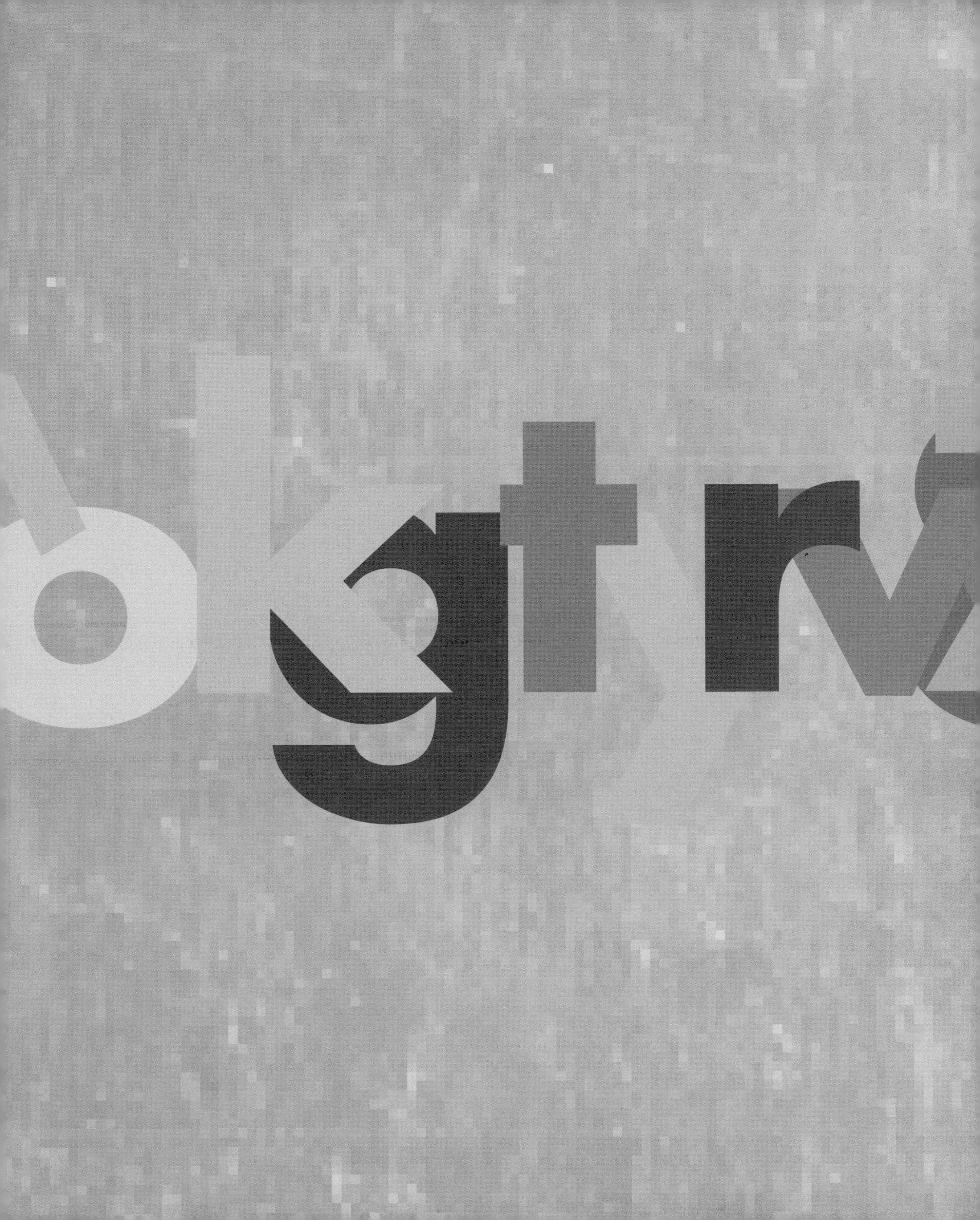

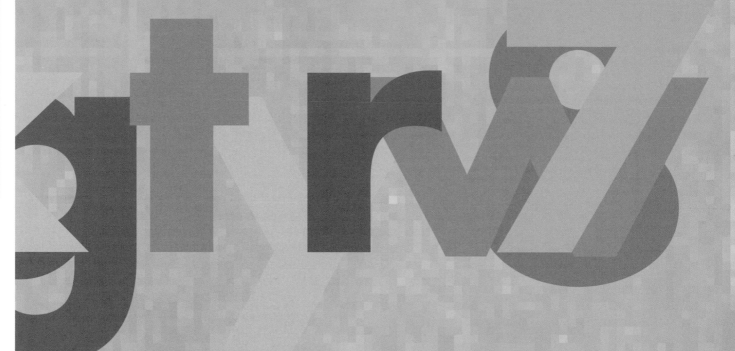

CLIENT

PROJECT DESCRIPTION

DATE

The National Museum of Photography,
Film and Television's Digital Frontiers Gallery.

THE NATIONAL MUSEUM OF PHOTOGRAPHY, FILM AND TELEVISION-BRADFORD
ART GALLERY
DECEMBER 1999

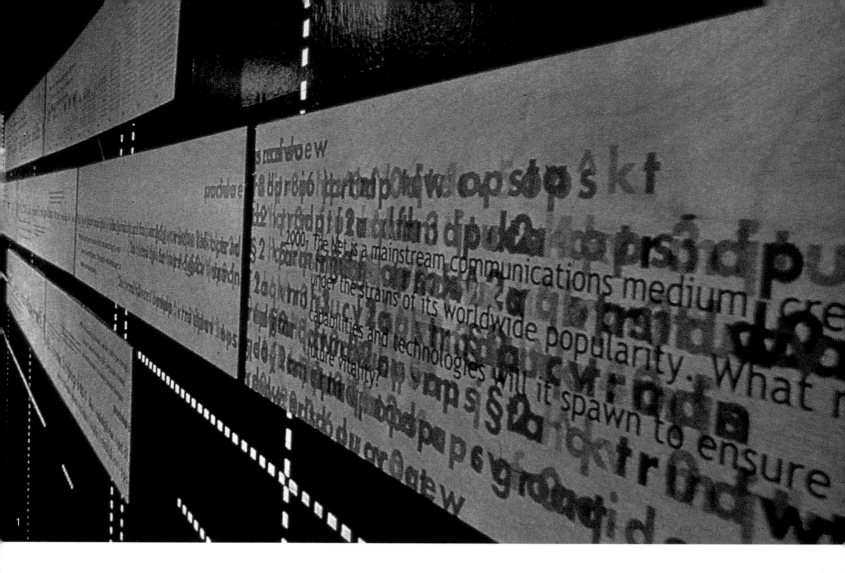

2000: The Net is a mainstream communications medium ... under the strains of its worldwide popularity. What ... capabilities and technologies will it spawn to ensure ... future vitality?

1 Text panels vary in execution technique—from the application of trebuched bold stencils using 3M Scotchlite reflective liquid to using galvanized steel sheet screen printed with two color graphics to illustrate the Net History.

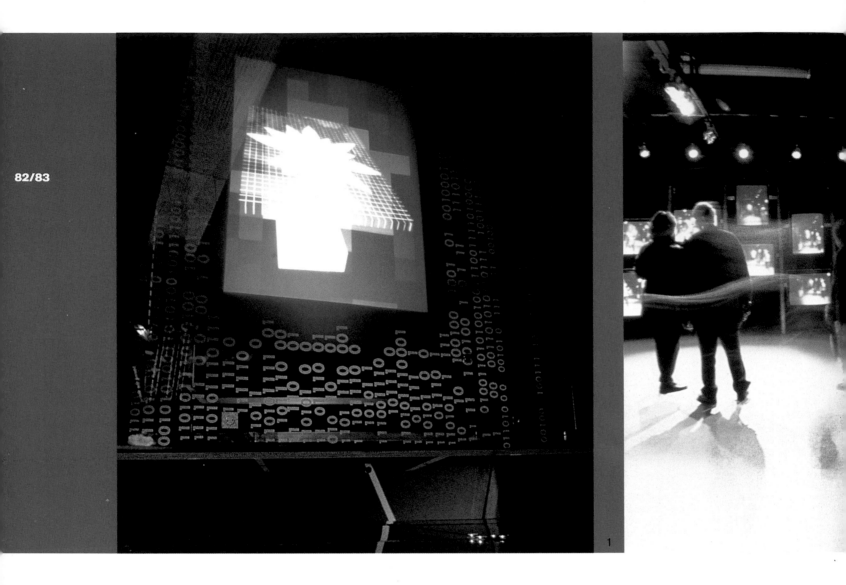

1

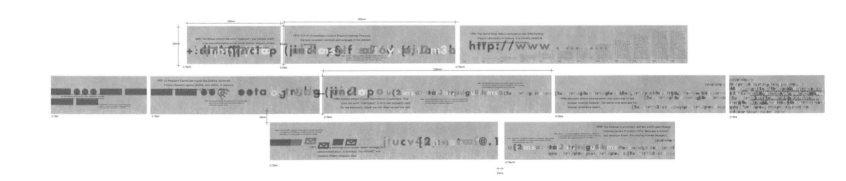

2

3

1 The Bits and Bytes exhibition is a large cube box that shows projects in an animated sequence explaining the basic differences between hardware and software.

2 In the foreground, the axis line of a parallelogram runs between the ceiling, walls, and floors. The background installation by the Japanese artist Toshi Iawi illustrates how computers process information. Eight monitors and cameras are hung off an angled steel framework.

3 At Toshio Iawi's "Another Time, Another Space," visitors are captured on camera, their image is processed on the way to the screens and morphed so that heads become interchanged with another spectator's body.

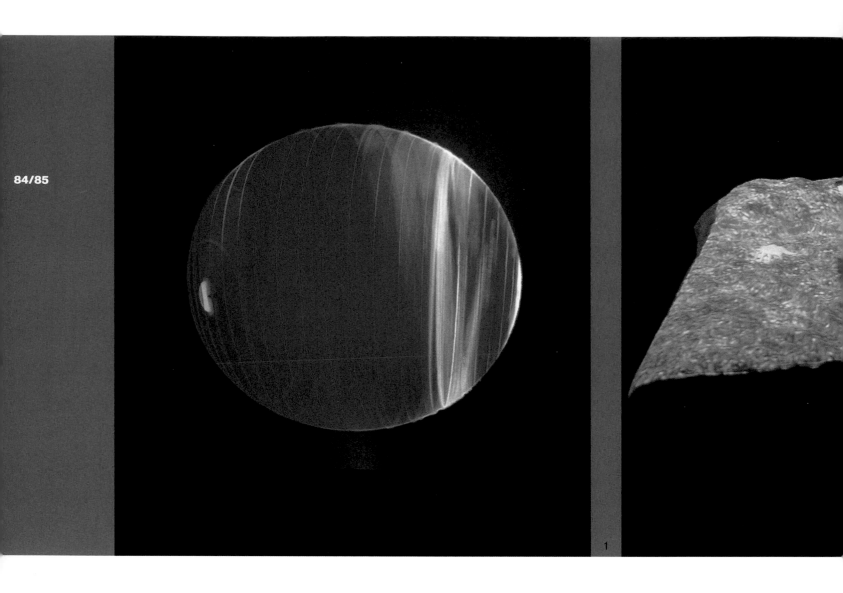

1

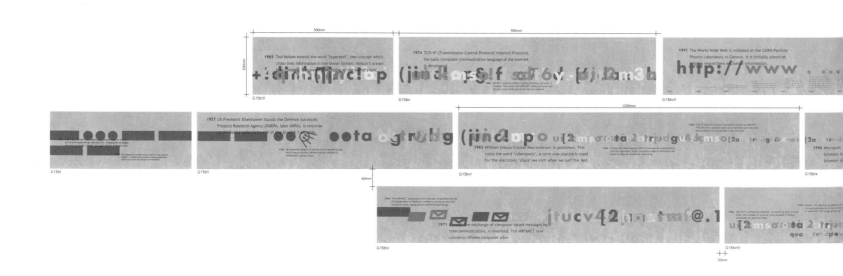

1965 Ted Nelson invents the word "hypertext", the concept which cross-links information in non-linear fashion. Nelson's dream is to put the whole of the world's text...

G15biii

1974 TCP/IP (Transmission Control Protocol/Internet Protocol), the basic computer communication language of the Internet, is developed.

G15bv

1991 The World Wide Web is initiated at the CERN Particle Physics Laboratory in Geneva. It is initially aimed at helping researchers exchange information.

G15bvii

G15bi

1957 US President Eisenhower founds the Defence Advanced Projects Research Agency (DARPA, later ARPA), in response to the launch by the Soviet Union of Sputnik 1.

G15bii

1983 William Gibson's novel Neuromancer is published. This coins the word "cyberspace", a term now popularly used for the electronic "place" we visit when we surf the Net.

G15bvi

1996 Microsoft...
browser...

G15bix

1971 E-mail, the exchange of computer-based messages by telecommunication, is invented. The ARPANET now connects fifteen computer sites.

G15biv

G15bviii

500mm 900mm 200mm 1200mm 60mm 20mm

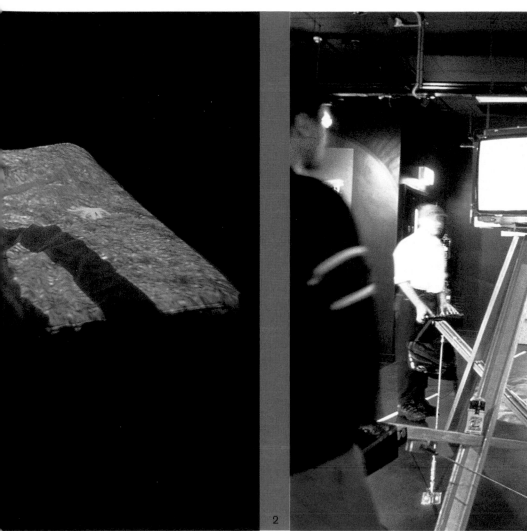

2

3

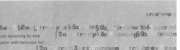

G15bx

1 For 'Ride the Byte,' Art & Com created a sphere to represent a virtual earth. The activities of the user weave a visual representation of the Internet's communication pattern.

2 The Berlin-based UK artist Paul Sermon's installation is a dramatic interpretation of video conferencing techniques. Two beds are connected by a live two-way digital link. Prerecorded imagery is mixed into the footage to add to the dream-like quality of the piece.

3 Network Games explore the preconceived notions that computer games are largely violent and exploitative. Visitors are invited to play at one of the chassis monitors that sit on galvanized steel framework console units. Tension cables brace the triangular structure.

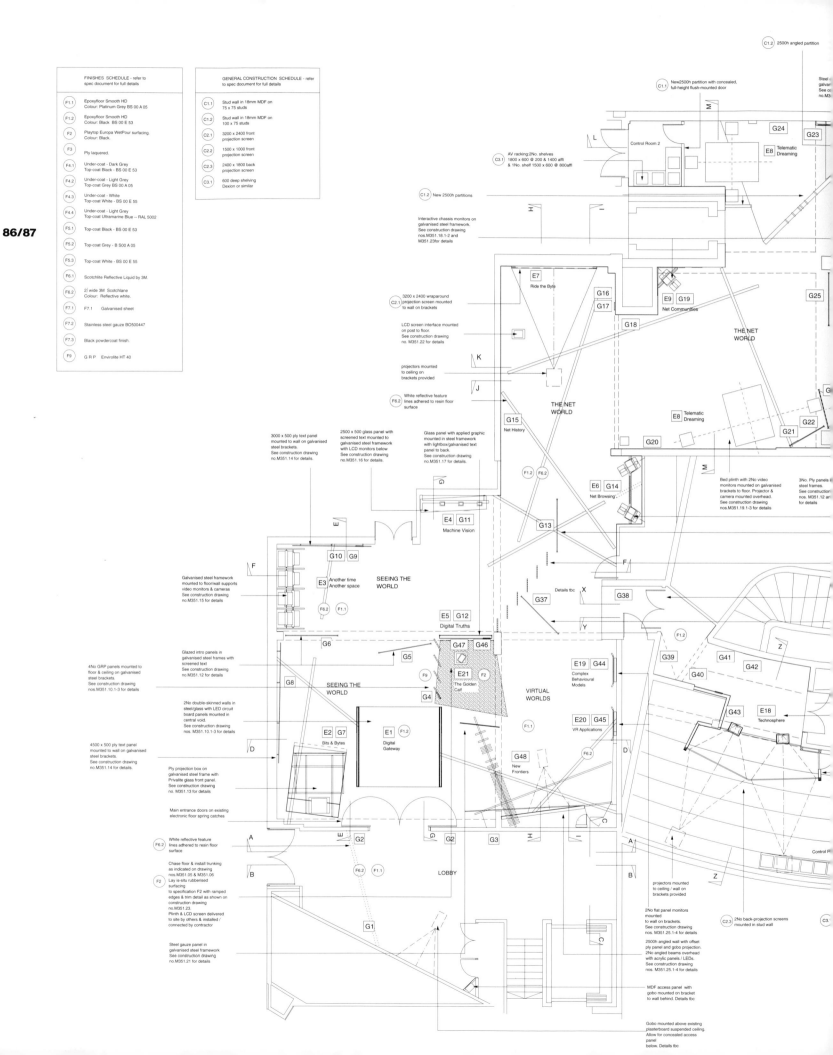

FINISHES SCHEDULE - refer to spec document for full details

- (F1.1) Epoxyfloor Smooth HD Colour: Platinum Grey BS 00 A 05
- (F1.2) Epoxyfloor Smooth HD Colour: Black BS 00 E 53
- (F2) Playtop Europa WetPour surfacing. Colour: Black.
- (F3) Ply laquered.
- (F4.1) Under-coat - Dark Grey Top-coat Black - BS 00 E 53
- (F4.2) Under-coat - Light Grey Top-coat Grey BS 00 A 05
- (F4.3) Under-coat - White Top-coat White - BS 00 E 55
- (F4.4) Under-coat - Light Grey Top-coat Ultramarine Blue -- RAL 5002
- (F5.1) Top-coat Black BS 00 E 53
- (F5.2) Top-coat Grey - B S00 A 05
- (F5.3) Top-coat White - BS 00 E 55
- (F6.1) Scotchlite Reflective Liquid by 3M.
- (F6.2) 2ʺ wide 3M Scotchlane Colour: Reflective white.
- (F7.1) F7.1 Galvanised sheet
- (F7.2) Stainless steel gauze BO500447
- (F7.3) Black powdercoat finish.
- (F9) G R P Envirolite HT 40

GENERAL CONSTRUCTION SCHEDULE - refer to spec document for full details

- (C1.1) Stud wall in 18mm MDF on 75 x 75 studs
- (C1.2) Stud wall in 18mm MDF on 100 x 75 studs
- (C2.1) 3200 x 2400 front projection screen
- (C2.2) 1500 x 1000 front projection screen
- (C2.3) 2400 x 1800 back projection screen
- (C3.1) 600 deep shelving Dexion or similar

(C1.2) 2500h angled partition

(C1.1) New2500h partition with concealed, full-height flush-mounted door

Control Room 2

G24   G23

(E8) Telematic Dreaming

(C1.2) New 2500h partitions

AV racking: 2No. shelves (C3.1) 1800 x 600 @ 200 & 1400 affl & 1No. shelf 1500 x 600 @ 800affl

Interactive chassis monitors on galvanised steel framework. See construction drawing nos. M351.18.1-2 and M351.23 for details

(E7) Ride the Byte

(C2.1) 3200 x 2400 wraparound projection screen mounted to wall on brackets

LCD screen interface mounted on post to floor. See construction drawing no. M351.22 for details

projectors mounted to ceiling on brackets provided

(F6.2) White reflective feature lines adhered to resin floor surface

G16   G17

(E9) (G19) Net Communities

G18

THE NET WORLD

G25

THE NET WORLD

(E8) Telematic Dreaming

(G15) Net History

Glass panel with applied graphic mounted in steel framework with lightbox/galvanised text panel to back. See construction drawing no. M351.17 for details.

3000 x 500 ply text panel mounted to wall on galvanised steel brackets. See construction drawing no. M351.14 for details.

2500 x 500 glass panel with screened text mounted to galvanised steel framework with LCD monitors below See construction drawing no. M351.16 for details.

(F1.2) (F6.2)

G20

G21   G22

(E6) (G14) Net Browsing

Bed plinth with 2No video monitors mounted on galvanised brackets to floor. Projector & camera mounted overhead. See construction drawing nos. M351.19.1-3 for details

3No. Ply panels in galvanised steel frames. See construction nos. M351.12 and for details

(E4) (G11) Machine Vision

G13

Galvanised steel framework mounted to floor/wall supports video monitors & cameras See construction drawing no. M351.15 for details

(E3) Another time Another space

SEEING THE WORLD

G10   G9

Details tbc (X)

(G37)

(E5) (G12) Digital Truths

G38

(F1.2)

(F6.2) (F1.1)

Glazed intro panels in galvanised steel frames with screened text See construction drawing no. M351.12 for details

G6

G5

(G47) (G46)

(E21) (F2) The Golden Calf

(F9)

VIRTUAL WORLDS

(E19) (G44) Complex Behavioural Models

G39

G41   G42

G40

(Z)

4No GRP panels mounted to floor & ceiling on galvanised steel brackets. See construction drawing nos. M351.10.1-3 for details

G8

SEEING THE WORLD

G4

(E20) (G45) VR Applications

(F1.1)

(E18) Technosphere

G43

2No double-skinned walls in steel/glass with LED circuit board panels mounted in central void. See construction drawing nos. M351.10.1-3 for details

(E2) (G7) Bits & Bytes

(E1) (F1.2) Digital Gateway

(F6.2)

4500 x 500 ply text panel mounted to wall on galvanised steel brackets. See construction drawing no. M351.14 for details.

(G48) New Frontiers

Ply projection box on galvanised steel frame with Privalite glass front panel. See construction drawing no. M351.13 for details

Main entrance doors on existing electronic floor spring catches

(F6.2) White reflective feature lines adhered to resin floor surface

(F2) Chase floor & install trunking as indicated on drawing nos. M351.05 & M351.06 Lay is-situ rubberised surfacing to specification F2 with ramped edges & trim detail as shown on construction drawing no. M351.23. Plinth & LCD screen delivered to site by others & installed / connected by contractor

Steel gauze panel in galvanised steel framework See construction drawing no. M351.21 for details

LOBBY

G1

G2   G3

(F6.2) (F1.1)

projectors mounted to ceiling / wall on brackets provided

2No flat panel monitors mounted to wall on brackets. See construction drawing nos. M351.25.1-4 for details

(C2.3) 2No back-projection screens mounted in stud wall

2500h angled wall with offset ply panel and gobo projection. 2No angled beams overhead with acrylic panels / LEDs. See construction drawing nos. M351.25.1-4 for details

MDF access panel with gobo mounted on bracket to wall behind. Details tbc

Gobo mounted above existing plasterboard suspended ceiling. Allow for concealed access panel below. Details tbc

Control Room

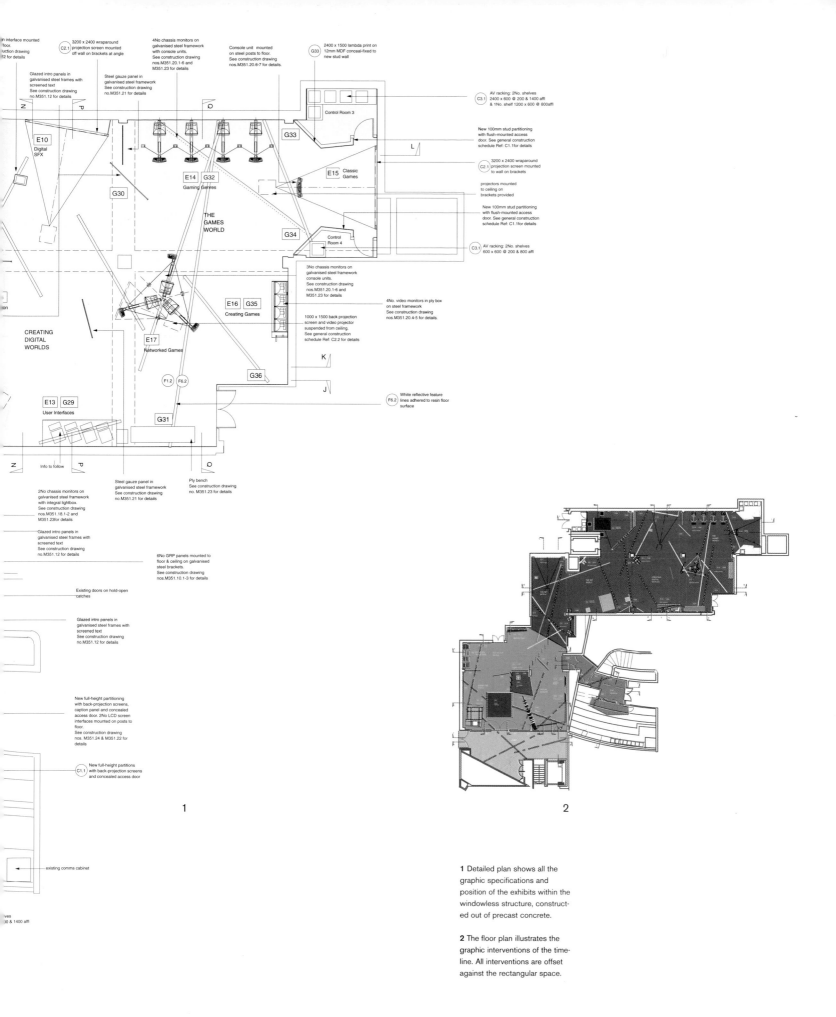

in interface mounted
... floor.
...ction drawing
...2 for details

Glazed intro panels in
galvanised steel frames with
screened text
See construction drawing
no.M351.12 for details

(C2.1) 3200 x 2400 wraparound
projection screen mounted
off wall on brackets at angle

Steel gauze panel in
galvanised steel framework
See construction drawing
no.M351.21 for details

4No chassis monitors on
galvanised steel framework
with console units.
See construction drawing
nos.M351.20.1-6 and
M351.23 for details

Console unit mounted
on steel posts to floor.
See construction drawing
nos.M351.20.6-7 for details.

(G33) 2400 x 1500 lambda print on
12mm MDF conceal-fixed to
new stud wall

E10
Digital
SFX

G30

Control Room 3

G33

E14 G32
Gaming Genres

E15 Classic
Games

(C3.1) AV racking: 2No. shelves
2400 x 600 @ 200 & 1400 affl
& 1No. shelf 1200 x 600 @ 800affl

New 100mm stud partitioning
with flush-mounted access
door. See general construction
schedule Ref: C1.1for details

L

THE
GAMES
WORLD

(C2.1) 3200 x 2400 wraparound
projection screen mounted
to wall on brackets

projectors mounted
to ceiling on
brackets provided

G34

Control
Room 4

New 100mm stud partitioning
with flush-mounted access
door. See general construction
schedule Ref: C1.1for details

(C3.1) AV racking: 2No. shelves
600 x 600 @ 200 & 800 affl

3No chassis monitors on
galvanised steel framework
console units.
See construction drawing
nos.M351.20.1-6 and
M351.23 for details

4No. video monitors in ply box
on steel framework
See construction drawing
nos.M351.20.4-5 for details.

E16 G35
Creating Games

1000 x 1500 back projection
screen and video projector
suspended from ceiling.
See general construction
schedule Ref: C2.2 for details

CREATING
DIGITAL
WORLDS

E17
Networked Games

K

F1.2 F6.2

G36

J

(F6.2) White reflective feature
lines adhered to resin floor
surface

E13 G29
User Interfaces

G31

N P O

Info to follow

Steel gauze panel in
galvanised steel framework
See construction drawing
no.M351.21 for details

Ply bench
See construction drawing
no. M351.23 for details

2No chassis monitors on
galvanised steel framework
with integral lightbox.
See construction drawing
nos.M351.18.1-2 and
M351.23for details

Glazed intro panels in
galvanised steel frames with
screened text
See construction drawing
no.M351.12 for details

6No GRP panels mounted to
floor & ceiling on galvanised
steel brackets.
See construction drawing
nos.M351.10.1-3 for details

Existing doors on hold-open
catches

Glazed intro panels in
galvanised steel frames with
screened text
See construction drawing
no.M351.12 for details

New full-height partitioning
with back-projection screens,
caption panel and concealed
access door. 2No LCD screen
interfaces mounted on posts to
floor.
See construction drawing
nos. M351.24 & M351.22 for
details

(C1.1) New full-height partitions
with back-projection screens
and concealed access door

existing comms cabinet

...ves
...00 & 1400 affl

1

2

1 Detailed plan shows all the
graphic specifications and
position of the exhibits within the
windowless structure, constructed out of precast concrete.

2 The floor plan illustrates the
graphic interventions of the time-
line. All interventions are offset
against the rectangular space.

| | PRINCIPAL | GRAEME WILLIAMSON | LOCATION | LONDON | YEAR FOUNDED | 1997 |
| | | ZOE SMITH | | | | |

24/seven trawl the city for inspiration. It's the discarded spaces and interstitial territories of remnants of past lives, reflected in textures and surfaces left behind in the urban fabric that the practice draws on. Formed in 1997, 24/seven has completed a series of projects: an office for Tomato in the heart of London, a loft, a hairdresser's salon, and the redesign of the bar at London's contemporary arts center, the ICA.

When invited to design the ICA bar in London, 24/seven set out to explore the relationship between appropriated objects and the highly specified object. The graphic design practice Brain Child Décor (BCD) was invited to join in the project because 24/seven felt BCD had a similiar design philosophy. BCD uses the environment as a design source, searching for architectural salvage, appropriating objects, and applying the results to a two-dimensional surface. The reverse process is also used: in an interview BCD gave in London's music and cultural magazine *Sleaze Nation* parts of the discussion were printed, increased in scale, and pasted onto public areas of the city to create a site-specific installation. BCD considers the design process a result of many happy accidents, taking graphics beyond its illustrative purpose into a new field of design.

CLIENT
PROJECT DESCRIPTION
DATE

The Bar at ICA

ICA
BAR INTERIOR DESIGN
1999

1

2

3

4

1 Urinal slabs clad the bar. The standardized items are fixed onto the old bar using split battens and are sealed with mastic joints.

2 A recessed shelf houses the bar's spirits. The wall is constructed of plywood stacked so that the edge of the plywood is revealed.

3 Exposed galvanized steel electrical ducting is used to supply stove lights.

4 The drinking area of the restaurant is separated from the quieter eating spaces, as seen from the mezzanine floor.

Situated on two floors, the ICA Bar was in need of a complete design refurbishment. 24/seven specified fireclay urinal slabs to form the new bar top and front to give a pure and utilitarian aesthetic. The warmth of the exposed plywood backdrop counteracts the cool ceramic of the urinal. The urinal slabs are standardized objects selected from the British sanitary ware catalogue, Armitage Shanks.

The perimeter seating is based on a doctor's waiting room sofa upholstered in red Rolls Royce leather. Behind this is a backlit hexalite screen that acts as an in-house billboard communicating future events taking place at the ICA. This material continues along the side of the staircase catching the movement of occupants and at the same time forms an edge to the new steel and laminated plywood balustrading. Behind the hexalite panels is a series of graphic panels designed by BCD. The hexalite is a sandwich board made up of two sheets of GRP with an aluminum honeycomb core. The images become pixilated through the material.

1

2

1 Designed by 24/seven, the tables are constructed of exposed edge plywood, in a CNC cut-shape. Twenty pieces are laminated together to make one table. The top is then spray finished in clear lacquer.

2 The matching benches, in red Rolls Royce leather, complete the designers' vision of an integrated interior

Klinik Hairdresser

CLIENT ANNE FORSLING
PROJECT DESCRIPTION SALON INTERIOR DESIGN
DATE SEPTEMBER 1998

1

2

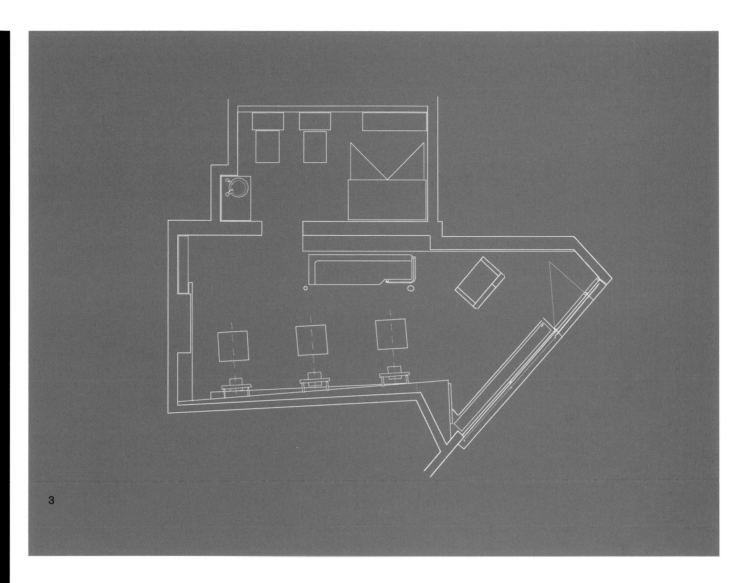

3

1 The narrow site of the Klinik Haridresser, which previously operated as a shop, as seen at night accentuates the clinical hues associated with operating theaters.

2 The space has been divided into three volumes: the central aisle that is articulated with three CCTV cameras; the wall with the mounted mirrors and monitors; and the waiting area.

3 The floor plan illustrates the oblique angle of the street façade and the compact nature of the site.

For the Klinik hairdressing salon in London's East End, 24/seven focused on one key concept—to create a clinical space that adhered to the highly mannered activity of hairdressing. This was applied to all aspects of the design from the furnishings down to the signage and all graphic identity, such as business cards and letter heads.

Influence was drawn on medical aesthetics to create an uncluttered and highly functional space with a degree of theatricality. Emphasis was placed on the vanity of the customer and to allow the client a degree of control over the environment. This is manifested in the positioning of CCTV cameras above each chair. An image is then relayed to the monitors at the base of each mirror. This allows a simultaneous double view of the head—one directly in front (the mirror) and one at the side through the monitor. The idea plays on the fascination of viewing a detached image of oneself from the perspective of an observer, so simultaneously one is the observer and also the observed.

Graeme Williamson describes his approach to the design as "treating the site as a surface similar to the methodology used in graphic design. The design of graphics adheres to the margins on the layout of the page, offsetting of color and color balance and how objects will be read side by side. We applied this concept to the designed space."

1

2

4

1 The digital clock blends with the space, mirroring the architecture's precision with time as the minutes flick by.

2 The slim furnishings reflect the building's narrow site. The introduction of curved steel bars breaks the geometry of the interior.

3 The rear wall divides the salon from the wet area. The chaise lounge upholstered in white leather combines luxury with functionality.

4 An example of the Klinik's letterhead.

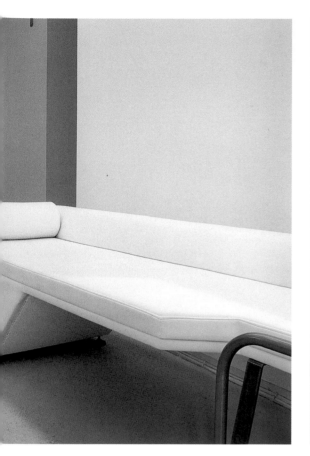

3

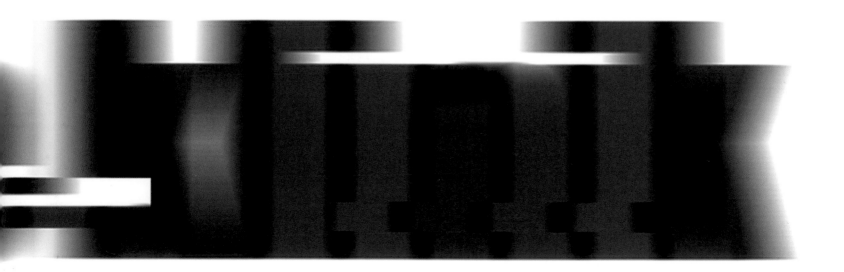

1

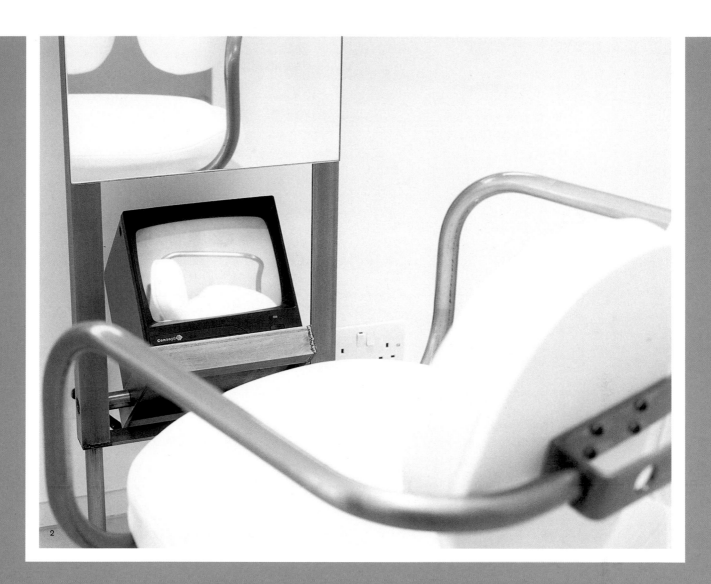

2

1 Three CCTV cameras are suspended from the four meter-high-ceiling. The images captured on the cameras are transmitted in real time.

2 A close-up of the viewing sequence. The client's face is reflected in the mirror and, in turn, the activities going on behind the client are relayed to the monitor via the suspended CCTV cameras.

**The Designers Republic with
Branson Coates Architecture**

PRINCIPAL	REPUBLIC: IAN ANDERSON	LOCATION	REPUBLIC: SHEFFIELD	YEAR FOUNDED	REPUBLIC: 1984
	B/C: NIGEL COATES DOUG BRANSON		LONDON		B/C: 1985

The Designers Republic (DR) hit out at consumer complacency with its own brand of polemical designs. The company's trademarks—the recycling of culture, appropriation of corporate logos, and ability to keep ahead—have made it one of the most copied design houses in the UK and all of this from a studio in the heart of England's now defunct steel manufacturing center, Sheffield.

But location does not matter anymore. Established in 1984, DR's designs have spanned the transition from traditional media to Mac-based design. The firm has built up a client base working with companies in the United States, Europe and Japan.

DR launched itself with the design of record sleeves. One of its most talked about covers, POP WILL EAT ITSELF, epitomised its work featuring the bastardisations of corporate logos—most notably the ripped off Pepsi logo. If there is one consistent message that DR wants to put across, it is to provoke the viewer into asking questions. From record sleeve covers to designing the graphics for computer games developer Psygnosis, to designing in-game visuals, typefaces, and logos, DR is moving into the digital realm. When asked which programs DR used Ian Anderson lists his favourites, "lots of Photoshop and Freehand, Illustrator? The tool of the devil."

In 1998, DR was asked to collaborate with the architects Branson Coates to design the interior of a sushi bar in London's Canary Wharf situated in the Docklands, an area of regeneration unrestricted by planning rules. Anderson describes the transition from two-dimensional work into the three-dimensional sphere as "a refreshing break from purely hands-on design... Rather it's about creating the entire ambience of a space. Interiors are something that we have been interested in. We are working more and more on projects that apply our graphic style into areas which are not specifically print orientated, such as the new Garbage video or the exterior for a promotional wagon for a fast-food company."

The collaboration was an ideal match. Branson Coates are known for their popular approach to architecture, drawing on the city and populist forms of entertainment to inform their design. Embracing expressive forms, Cafe Bongo, designed in Tokyo, by Branson Coates has an airline crashing into the facade and more recent work, such as the National Centre for Popular Music in Sheffield, is composed of four drums.

1

2

3

4

飲み放題

→ ◯ 南北線
Namboku Line
約300m先 Ahead

← ← ← のりかえ
Transfer

1

Moshi Moshi Sushi

MOSHI MOSHI SUSHI
FAST FOOD RESTAURANT
APRIL 1998

2

The idea behind Moshi Moshi Sushi is to simulate the state of a microcosm of Tokyo, by focusing the design on elements of the Tokyo transportation system and evoking the perpetually animated atmosphere that expresses a city in a constant state of flux.

The space is composed primarily of a sloping conveyor belt that roller coasters its way around carrying sushi, while a high-level track above convoys transparent spheres containing customized plastic sushi in the form of cutting-edge transport. DR intrinsically relies on typography, form, color, texture, style, and the use of as tools to express the content of design.

トウキョウ **INTER NATIONAL**

MMS³

The logo created for Moshi Moshi Sushi.

デザイナーズリパブリック

1 The food preparation takes part in the central area that is separated by the conveyor belt, which acts as a bound-ary between the preparation and the eating zones. A cor-rugated wall screens the restroom entrances from the main space and also acts as an advertising billboard.

2 The conveyor belt circulates the sushi dishes that are selected by the customers. A giant stainless-steel tea urn takes a promi-nent position against one of the Designer Republic's wall graphics.

3 An example of the wall graphics demonstrates DR's love of iconographics. The quote 'More tea equals greater productivity' is appro-priated from a Japanese advertisement.

たくさんのお茶＝より高い生産性

MORE TEA=GREATER PRODUCTIVITY

In 1997 the design duo Gerard Hadders and Barbara Dijkhuis—working under the practice name Buro Lange Haven (BLH)—was asked to develop a new identifying trademark of typography for the Dutch postal buildings, PTT Post. Boasting a long history of commissioning innovative design, the Dutch Postal service wanted a new company logo and corporate identity that could be fully integrated with the new architectural structures.

The main objective for this identity was flexibility so that it could be applied to a variety of products and buildings. Buro Lange Haven set up a sister company that would solely develop this typographical system, naming it System Typography Integrated Program (STIP).

The designers have a varied background in the visual arts. Hadders, who graduated as a fine artist and photographer, has developed a distinctive style and produced a prolific and varied amount of work. In 1979 he co-founded *Hard Werken* Magazine, a beautifully executed alternative magazine for graphic arts and has been on the editorial board for *Eye Magazine*. BLH's work has been exhibited widely; *Hard Werken* was included in the exhibition "Les Mots and Les Images," at the Centre Pompidou in Paris and at the Stedelijk Museum in Amsterdam and brought BLH into the field of exhibition design and site specific art. Volkswagen invited them to design an installation for its headquarters.

BLH's history of experimentation with typography made the group ideal to create the typography system and corporate identity for the PTT Post building. PTT were commissioning a group of high-tech modular buildings that would be situated in business parks in the vicinity of traffic intersections. The buildings are glazed, shed-type, fast-track constructions. The visibility system is intended to provide an identity so that the office would stand out from the other industrial sheds and to subtly lift the architecture from the anonymity of the business park.

CPZ architects in Delft designed the buildings in which the universal visibility system was to be integrated.

The pattern that forms the foundation of the system is based on a matrix of dots. The dots are 75 mm in diameter manufactured using retro-reflecting prismatic foil. The dots are small enough to be clearly perceptible close up and large enough to create a monumental image at a distance.

When deciding on the design of the corporate identity, use had to be made in broad terms of the existing PTT Post house-style. The "ball matrix" applied in the colors of the PTT logo proved to be very suitable for this purpose. By dotting the PTT logo in different sizes and variations on the ball matrix, a vocabulary is created that can be used as a database when designing the facade of subsequent buildings. This database offers endless variations within the given framework. Logos other than that of PTT Post can be built up from the main matrix system without detracting from the visual harmony of the building.

2

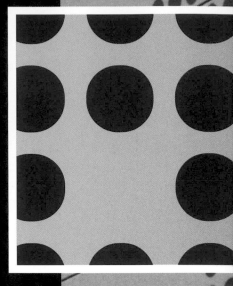

CLIENT
PROJECT DESCRIPTION
DATE

System Typography Integrated Programme

DUTCH POST OFFICE
EXTERIOR AND INTERIOR GRAPHICS FOR DUTCH POST OFFICES
1999

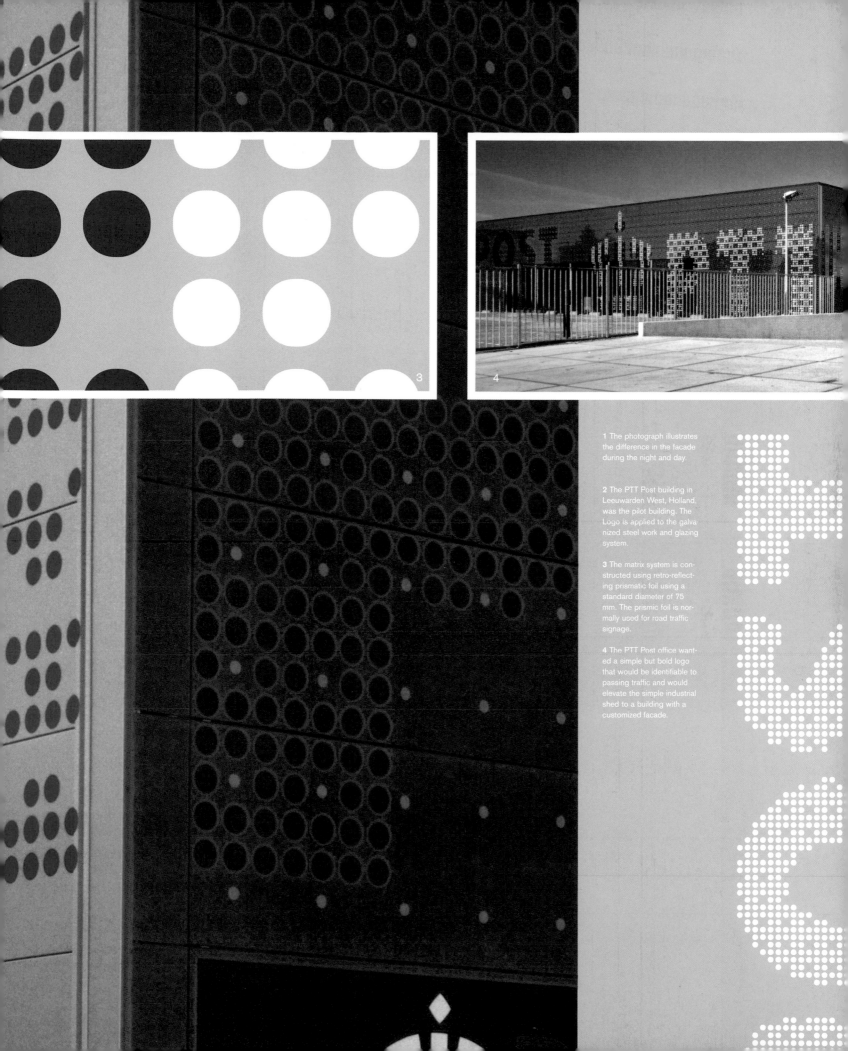

3

4

1 The photograph illustrates the difference in the facade during the night and day.

2 The PTT Post building in Leeuwarden West, Holland, was the pilot building. The Logo is applied to the galvanized steel work and glazing system.

3 The matrix system is constructed using retro-reflecting prismatic foil using a standard diameter of 75 mm. The prismic foil is normally used for road traffic signage.

4 The PTT Post office wanted a simple but bold logo that would be identifiable to passing traffic and would elevate the simple industrial shed to a building with a customized facade.

1 The building has no external lights to illuminate the facade; instead lighting poles in the parking lot refract light onto the dot matrixes.

2 The dots that form the matrix of design are manufactured in continuous roles and then cut out using lettering stencils.

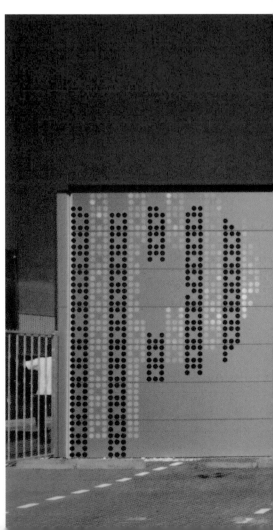

1

2

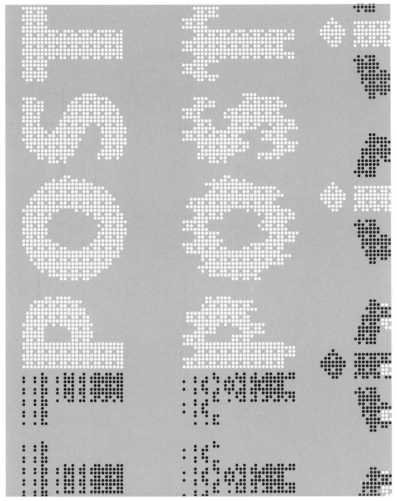

1 The standardized glass-
and wood-frame partition
walls are decorated with
the matrix system to provide
a degree of privacy. Over-
scaled images of people in
action are stuck onto the
glazed walls.

2 The logos of the
PTT Post are translated
through the application
of the matrix system.

| PRINCIPAL | KLAUS WUERSCHINGER | LOCATION | BERLIN | YEAR FOUNDED | 1997 |
| | MICHAEL WEBER | | | | |

Orb Design expands and contracts to meet the demands of each project. The core team, consisting of two partners Klaus Wuerschinger and Michael Webel, established the studio in 1997. Projects range from graphic-based work to installations and architecture. One installation project titled Sperlhammer questioned the interface between the natural and the artificial within the historic setting of an abandoned glass grinding mill in Bavaria.

Three greenhouses clad with mirrors playing audiotapes evoked the sound of the once-functioning mill.

Amongst the company's architectural projects have included an industrial manufacturing hall in the Czech Republic and a secondary school in the south of Germany.

If there is one prevailing design objective that Orb adheres to it is to listen to the client's needs and respond by bringing its own clear vision of design. Orb uses the archaeology of the site and feeds this back into the design. Taking materials out of their normal context, the design team searches through catalog directories for industrial materials to incorporate into their projects. This no frills approach and pragmatism has meant that Orb has completed a remarkable number of buildings considering its

relatively young existence as a firm.
An office building in the South of Germany commissioned by the French manufacturer of car parts required a total design concept from architecture and interior design to signage. Bold precast concrete elements were introduced and etchings of the company's logo onto interior curved glass walls provided a smooth integration between architecture and corporate identity.

Orb Design Studio is based in Berlin, the appointed capital of Germany once the country underwent unification. The city is in a state of flux with the demand for apartments rising, which makes the firm ideally situated for applying its rich mix of design skills. Berlin's nineteenth-century boulevards house double courtyards built to reduce the amount of window openings onto the street frontage. Behind these

facades are expansive areas of light industrial space, constructed of steel frames and clad with ornamental stone and brickwork.

Orb converted one floor of one of these nineteenth-century buildings to operate as a live/work environment in Kreuzberg, a district that was formally part of East Berlin—the brief set out to create six workstations, two separate living areas and a wet area that would include the kitchen and bathroom. The second floor apartment runs the whole width of the building, looking onto courtyards on both the south and north sides with a total of 250 square meters. The building previously operated as a light industrial space, producing metalware, with two small toilet cubicles.

Kreuzberg Apartment

ORB DESIGN
APARTMENT - CONVERSION FROM LIGHT INDUSTRIAL SPACE TO LIVE/WORK.
JANUARY 2000

CLIENT
PROJECT DESCRIPTION
DATE

1

1 and 2 Double-glazed aluminium frames were ordered from a window manufacturer to provide a degree of privacy. Acoustically, the glazed partitions provide a screening from the public space but do not interfere with the open plan layout of the apartment.

Following Pages

1 The grand entrance is typical of many nineteenth-century light industrial buildings built in Berlin around the 1880's. The ornamentation in neo-classical style has been covered (in mesh) so as to discourage any nesting pigeons.

2 A detail of the shelving system that divides the workspace from the dining/meeting room area. All paints specified use organic pigment.

3 The kitchen is designed as a freestanding object set in the expanse of epoxy floor. High-density wood with a durable spray finish is used for the kitchen island. Three pendant Becker lights in the Bauhaus style emphasize the kitchen area.

4 Looking from east to west, one can see the marble effect on the floor as a result of the coats of resin. Ancillary rooms surround the main space on the east and west sides.

5 The original door to the apartment, constructed out of solid corrugated iron with a cast-iron handle, is still in place. The industrial nature of the entrance belies the residential retreat behind the heavy doors.

6 A detail of the original brickwork demonstrates the irregular placement of

the bricks. The walls are constructed of two layers of brick with a cavity between the brickwork.

7 The reflection of the epoxy resin on the floor is similar to the detail found from a reflection on glass.

8 A detail of the artificial rose set in a row of four to emphasise the linearity of the space.

Applying a graphic sensibility to demarcate the work and public zones, the floor was treated like a blank canvas onto which was poured a specialized floor finish, made up of layers of epoxy resin, alternating between transparent epoxy and red epoxy resin. Orb custom-designed furniture for these zoned work areas not exceeding 1.2 metres in height so as not to block any light from the south side. The space, therefore, is flooded with light and the floor's highly polished surface reflects the light even on a dull day. The private areas are screened off with the construction of double-glazed aluminium frames. The space operates ideally oscillating between the public and the private. Meetings can be held in the central area that doubles up as a dining room for entertaining.

1

2

5   6

PRINCIPAL | OLIVER SALWAY | LOCATION | LONDON | YEAR FOUNDED | 1995
CHRISTOPHER BAGOT
DANIEL EVANS

Softroom has been creating an arcadia of luxury architectural pads employing their skill at three-dimensional computer imaging. Supersonic dream pads or private jets with state of the art technology—spatial dreams come in all shapes and sizes. Commissioned by the magazine *Wallpaper* to create visions of luxury living, Softroom exploited the fact that these interiors would remain firmly on the glossy page.

Developed through three-dimensional computer tools, the images have been applied to advertising campaigns for clients such as the make-up company Accessorise, the German newspaper *Die Zeit* and the British Broadcasting Company. The team at Softroom are predominantly made up of architect/designers who graduated from the Bartlett School of Architecture and are adamant that their work should not be categorized.

The work for *Wallpaper* magazine helped to improve Softroom's public profile, although most people could not see any direct relation between what's on the magazine page and the interior of their own home. Softroom's director Oliver Salway interpreted *Wallpaper*'s brief with a lot of creative freedom: "The mandate from *Wallpaper* was very loose—one or two lines asking us to design a living based around the theme of travel; for example, a train carriage. We would go ahead and design a jet plane.

If you're doing a project that will only be seen on a magazine page you would be missing an opportunity if you did not free yourself from normal budgetary and structural constraints."

Softroom's first coup in the world of built projects came when they were invited to take part in a competition to design a shelter in a rural environment in north England. Competition was fierce with invited entries coming from international practices such as Future Systems and Alsop and Störmer. Softroom described the design process as providing a direct contrast from the predominantly graphic concerns of the *Wallpaper* projects. An image provided by the client of a panoramic view kickstarted the project. "We tried to recreate the view in the photograph and interpreted the landscape of the site as being quite unnatural due to the degree of artifice in the photograph," Salway said. "The project is a useful bridge, between a conceptual project

and a built project." The solution can be described as a merging of two building types, the folly and the cabin. Designed to provide shelter from the elements for passengers before they board the ferry at the lake in Kielder Forest, it takes on the air of a pavilion for the twenty-first century. The pavilion does not have to be a fully operational serviced construction but has to last the normal life span of a building—approximately twenty-five years—so practicalities had to be considered.

When asked what role the computer plays in informing Softroom's work, Salway replies "I am always wary of direct analogies with three-dimensional imaging programs on the computer and built projects, the computer allows a greater degree of freedom and opportunity to play with materials rather than a polyboard model. Once you are competent with the technology and it becomes part of your tool kit and palette, you want to start playing with that for real."

CLIENT
PROJECT DESCRIPTION
DATE

Kielder Belvedere Partnership

KIELDER PARTNERSHIP
BELVEDERE SHELTER FOR FERRY PASSENGERS
OCTOBER 1999

1

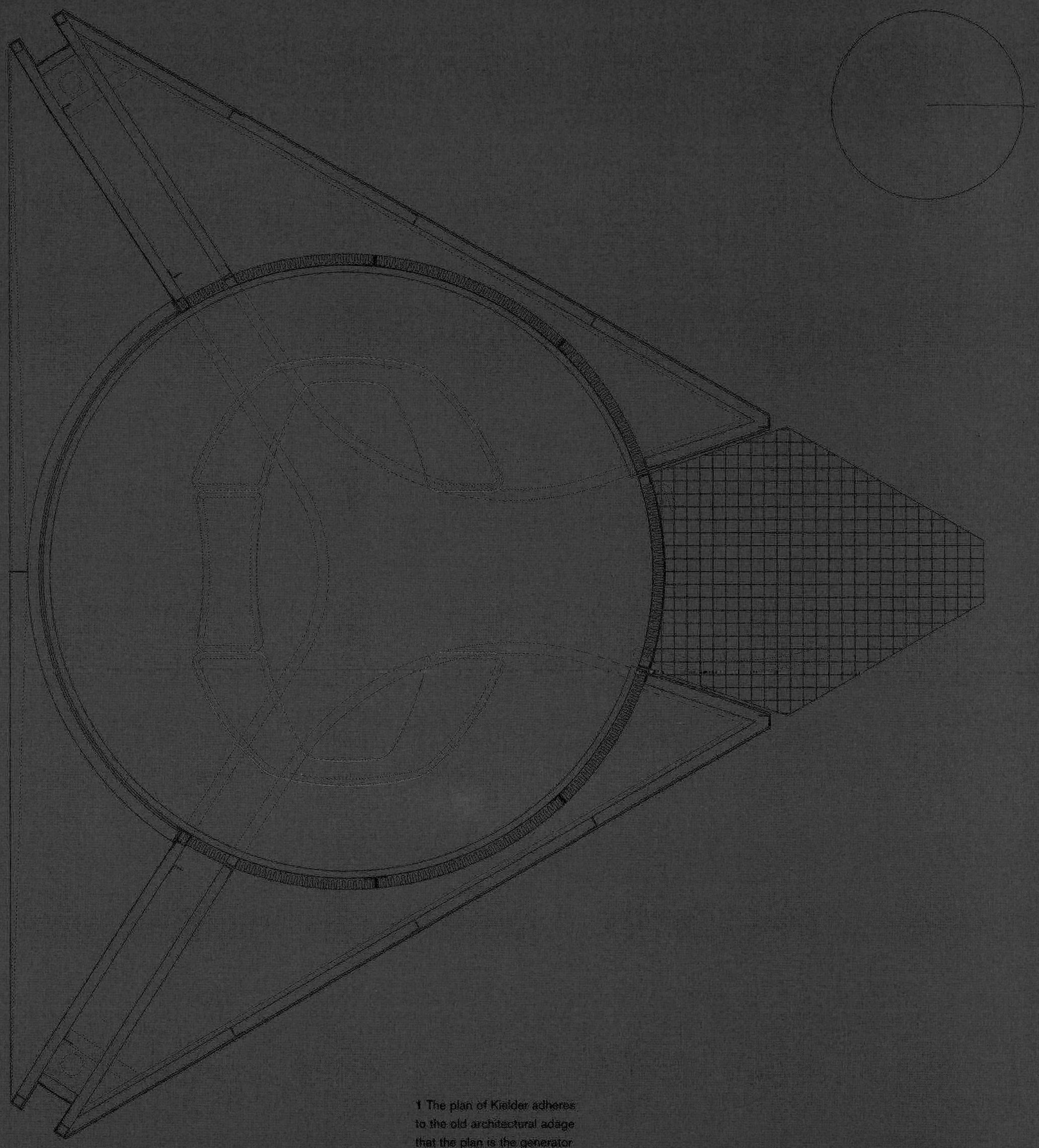

1 The plan of Kielder adheres
to the old architectural adage
that the plan is the generator
of the project and demon-
strates a graphic sensibility.

2 On the flank wall the stainless-steel skin maps the landscape onto the surface of the
building. Salway describes
the effect, "It is not about the
building disappearing but is
about changing the surface
like a changing wallpaper."

0   1   2   3   4m

9902/04 · KIELDER BELVEDERE : 3/4 VIEW SHOWING FRONT ELEVATION WITH SLOT WINDOW AND ETCHED STAINLESS STEEL CLADDING TO SIDES   ARCHITECTURE : SOFTROOM   CREDIT ESSENTIAL FOR PUBLICATION   PHOTOGRAPHY : KEITH PAISLEY

1   2

9902/08 – KIELDER BELVEDERE : DETAIL OF FRONT ELEVATION
CREDIT ESSENTIAL FOR PUBLICATION

4ARCHITECTURE : SOFTROOM
PHOTOGRAPHY : JOSEPHINE PLETTS

1 The plan shows the interior space and the structural roof elements. A yellow laminated, toughened glass skylight tops the building to allow sky gazing.

2 On the front of the building is an attempt to manifest the idea of the cone of vision stretching beyond one perspective point. A galvanized steel grating step has been cut to follow the building's line.

3 The rear window is constructed using polycarbonate.

9902/05 - KIELDER BELVEDERE : FRONT ELEVATION WITH SLOT WINDOW AND GOLDEN DRUM WITHIN   ARCHITECTURE : SOFTROOM   CREDIT ESSENTIAL FOR PUBLICATION   PHOTOGRAPHY : KEITH PAISLEY

9902/13 - KIELDER BELVEDERE   CONVEX MIRROR POLISHED STAINLESS STEEL FRONT ELEVATION   ARCHITECTURE : SOFTROOM   CREDIT ESSENTIAL FOR PUBLICATION   PHOTOGRAPHY : PETER SHARPE

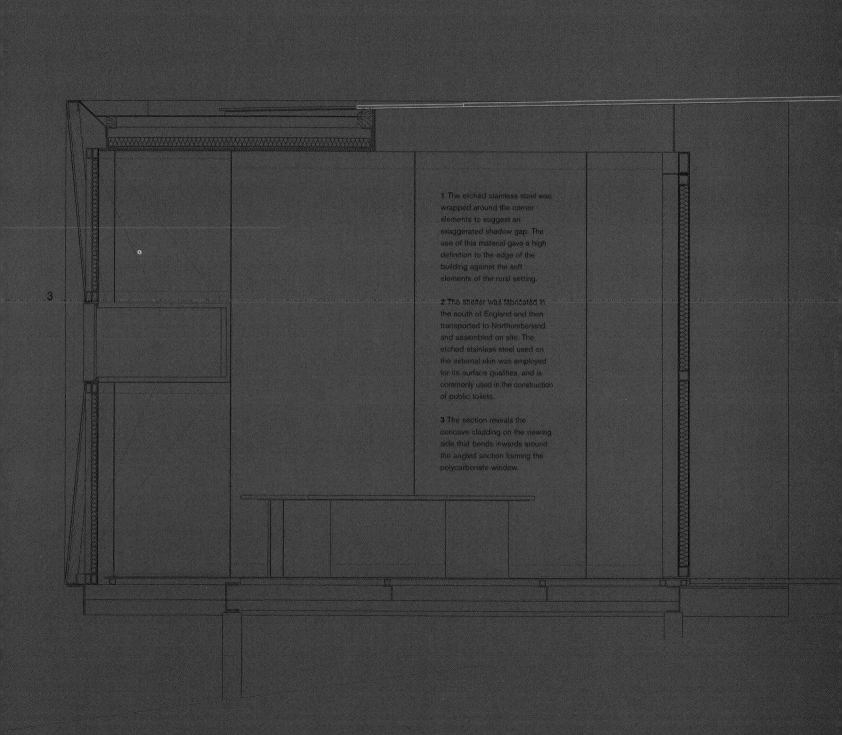

3

1 The etched stainless steel was
wrapped around the corner
elements to suggest an
exaggerated shadow gap. The
use of this material gave a high
definition to the edge of the
building against the soft
elements of the rural setting.

2 The shelter was fabricated in
the south of England and then
transported to Northumberland
and assembled on site. The
etched stainless steel used on
the external skin was employed
for its surface qualities, and is
commonly used in the construction
of public toilets.

3 The section reveals the
concave cladding on the viewing
side that bends inwards around
the angled section framing the
polycarbonate window.

CLIENT
PROJECT DESCRIPTION
DATE

Swiss Army Knife House

WALLPAPER MAGAZINE
LIVING SPACE
1997

The Swiss Army Knife house
was a conceptual design for
living commissioned by
Wallpaper magazine.
Furnishing elements can be
folded out of the main body
of the knife when required.

An interior visualization shows the foldout bar and seating area with compact low table. All the elements cantilever out of the body of the knife. The projects for *Wallpaper* were intended to be highly conceptual and graphic portrayals of futuristic living models.

| AGENCY/ DESIGNER | ARNOUD TRAAST EDITH GRUSON | LOCATION | SCHIEDAM, HOLLAND | YEAR FOUNDED | 1986 |

With Traast and Gruson's opening gambit, "We use clichés to attract attention," you know that these designers have a few tricks up their sleeve. Ambidextrous in their approach to solving design solutions and readiness to rid their work of design conventions, Traast and Gruson's designs are a delightful mix of entertainment and education.

Based in Holland, the partners who both started off studying graphic design and photography, are now excelling in the field of exhibition design, product presentation, and temporary spaces. Traast and Gruson, who claim that their designs aim to target anyone who's interested in change within the discipline of visual communication, do not have a recognizable signature. Each design is very much a response to the targeted audience.

"It's easy to read our exhibitions," Traast explains, "But we don't make the sort of books on legs that so many graphic designers resort to when designing an exhibition: blow up a couple of pages, affix them to panels and stick a couple of legs underneath. We always start with a space, which we exploit to the fullest. Our work is architectonic."

Deploying the Surrealist tactic of taking the ordinary and placing it in a quirky context, is a ploy to draw in the spectator. Once enticed, another level of information is revealed. The designers have worked together with Droog design, the Dutch presence that has introduced a refreshing aesthetic that combines good design with humour. For the 1999 Milan Furniture Fair Traast and Gruson worked together with Droog on two exhibitions, one for the high-market Danish audio-visual manufacturers Bang and Olfsen, the other for the German municipality, the Oranienbaum Estate.

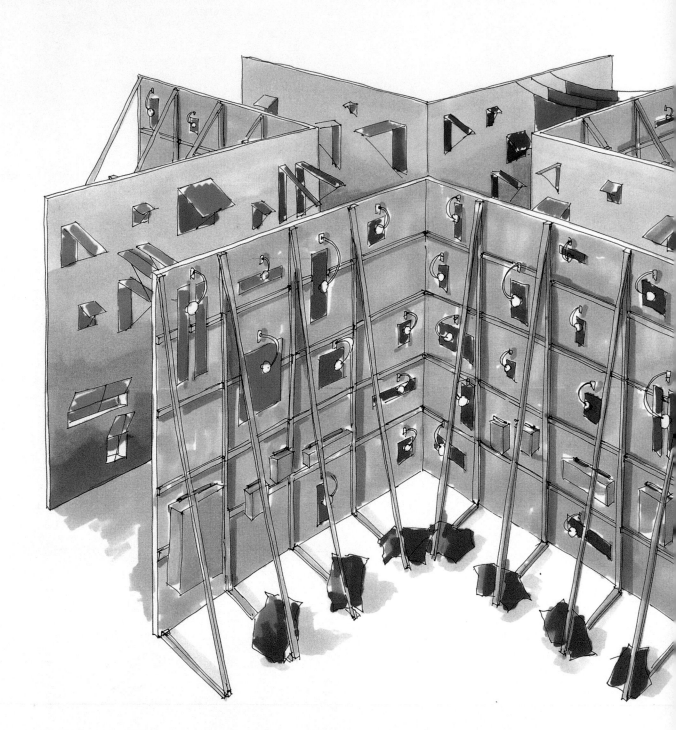

CLIENT
PROJECT DESCRIPTION
DATE

Signs in the Street

MILAN TRIENNIAL EXHIBITION
EXHIBITION DESIGN AND GRAPHICS
1992

1

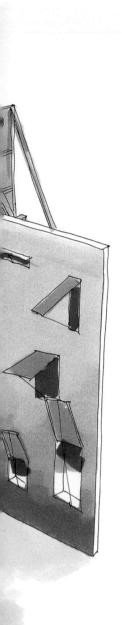

2

1 The illustration demonstrates the theatrical nature of the exhibition with the structure revealed, which actually becomes part of the exhibit.

2 The illustration shows a detail of the display boxes that are held open with stainless steel rods. The windows represent the domestic nature of mail that is an integral interface between post and recipient.

Holland's embracing of the benefits of good design is exemplified in its postal system, which asked Traast and Gruson to illustrate its design history for the eighteenth Triennial in Milan. The designers are strongly influenced by context, time, and subject and are adamant that their exhibitions should not be viewed as interchangeable. The exhibition "Signs in the Street," made reference to the narrow streets and washing lines that festoon Italian towns. Built as an intersection, the design featured two streets—one with historical features and the other representing a contemporary environment. The vivid colors exaggerate the theatricality of the space, which was further emphasized in the stage set construction. Viewers were invited to walk round the whole exhibition so that they could see explicitly how it was constructed. Sandbags prop up the wooden frame, giving the design a playful rough and ready finish.

ptt telecom
TUVW
ABCDEFGHIJKL
telefoon
NEDERLAND
POSTERIJEN

1

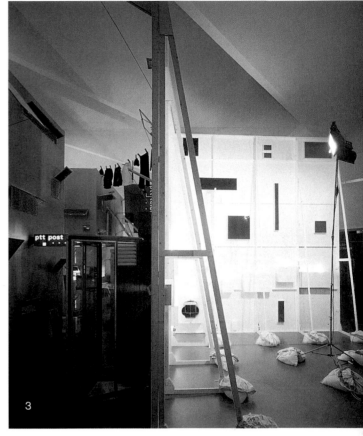

1 Street furniture has been installed in the artificial streets, with examples of post boxes and telephone boxes that demonstrate the evolution of the in-house design.

2 An example of a window that has been cut into the mock-up facades providing a view of a picture or model for the Royal PTT, the Dutch postal company.

3 The exhibition illustrates the Dutch postal company's design policy that has successfully created an identifiable image manifest in its architecture, graphics, and street furniture.

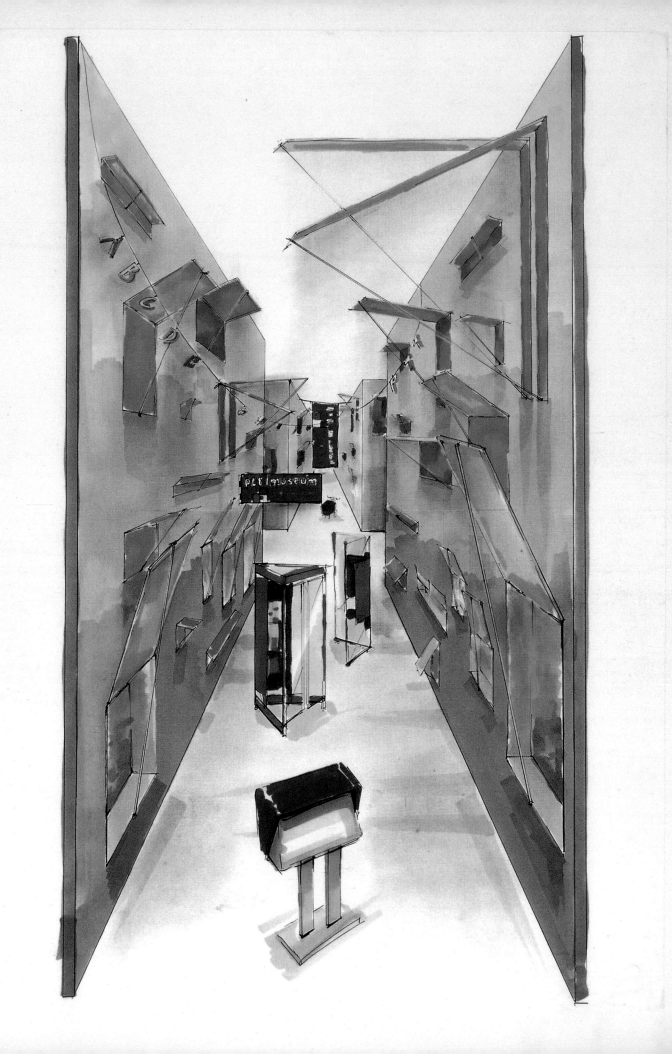

1 A preliminary sketch renders the space almost identical to the finished exhibition display.

2 Washing lines have been strung up between the building facades with the new uniforms of PTT hanging from the line.

Death Made Tangible

MUSEUM OF THE HAGUE
EXHIBITION DESIGN AND GRAPHICS
1999

1

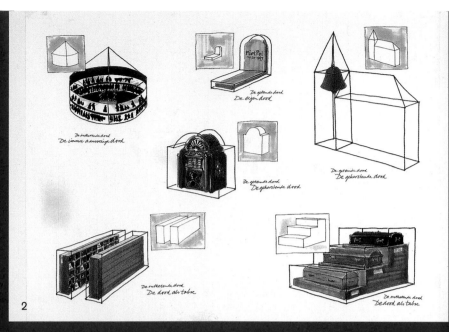

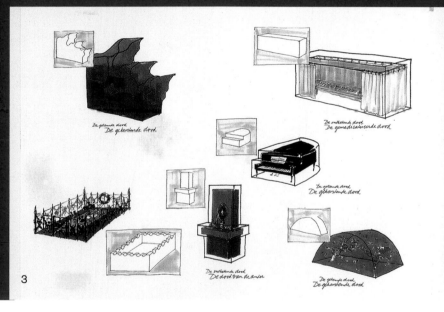

1 A temporary black box was constructed to house the exhibition. The boxes are abstractions of funereal objects such as a shrine, mausoleum, and grave stone. Painted in black—the color that allegorizes death—this contrasted sharply with the interior colour scheme.

2 and 3 Preliminary sketch illustrating the origin of the abstracted objects. Elaborate funeral objects such as coffins, tombstones, and altars are reduced to their silhouette image.

Of a more permanent nature than Signs in the Street, the second exhibition was commissioned by the Museum of the Hague. The exhibition's brief was to illustrate the 2,000-year history of how Dutch people relate to the void left by death and bereavement. Built to last for a period of several months, Traast and Gruson's approach here is different to a temporary exhibition. Specified finishes are more durable and materials more solid to reflect the exhibition's life expectancy. Treatment of subject matter is explored in more depth, with the premise that spectators may return to the exhibition for a second visit; therefore, the amount of information is

more complex. Traast and Gruson are very clear about defining the parameters of their discipline. When asked to comment on the involvement of the client in the design process, Gruson says: "I like to be presented with a problem and to take total responsibility for the solution."

"Death Made Tangible" uses abstractions of religious objects to chronicle the journey to death. The funereal objects include a shrine, mausoleum, and gravestone, painted black as an allegory to death. In the exhibition, text is left to a minimum.

1

2

3

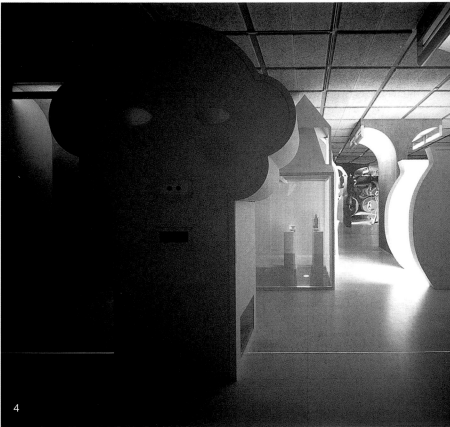

4

1 Objects are displayed not beside fused labels. Semi-transparent white tulle is used to cover the objects.

2 The circular exhibition case that can be viewed from either side. A hinged poly-carbonate door seals the cabinet.

3 The minimal amount of text is used. Instead of a "chronological history", the "historic concepts" that pro-vide a picture of Dutch fune-rary culture surrounding death is illustrated through objects and theatrical settings.

4 As visitors approach the objects, sensors are activated making the objects trans-parent and the items inside them visible. The sensual space provides a multi-sen-sory experience with the light, sounds, colours and temperature shifts.

5 A silhouette of a mourning person is reproduced on to the fabric that surrounds the free-standing freezers. The floor is drawn in the shape that blurs the separation of the ceiling and floor to give the illusion that they are working on an incline.

5

PRINCIPALS | **NIC CLEAR, DANNY VAIA,** | LOCATION | **LONDON** | YEAR FOUNDED | **1996**
JONNY HALIFAX, EZRA HOLLAND

The design leaders of General Lighting and Power (GLP) work hard and play hard. GLP apply its design skills to a range of media, advertising campaigns, television graphics, pop videos, and architecture. The practice's design delves into a broad cultural vocabulary from music iconography to architectural symbolism— a technique the practice calls sampling. Just as sampling hit the DJ scene back in the 1980s, the method has been adopted by the design world.

Trained in architecture, the four-man company see this as a strength—introducing the language of architectural drawing into their graphic work. In addition, the company claims that a large percentage of architecture is about communicating one's ideas through graphics; the presentation of a project often remains as paper architecture. In this case drawing is not used as a language of construction but as an art form of graphic communication. An advertising campaign for Peugeot used the now defunct dye-line architectural print for the advertising poster. A magazine advertisement promoted the release of an album of the original 1960s BBC music session recordings of the legendary band The Who, which took the iconographic imagery of the original promotional posters from 1965-70 and overlaid it with architectural conventions. "People try

and pigeonhole us it gives them a greater sense of control," says Nic Clear. GLP tries to dodge any categorization.

Technique is key to the practice's work. All projects—whether advertising, graphic, or architectural—are digitally based, moving with ease from two-dimensional packaging to animation programs and top-of-the-range digital editing software.

General Lighting and Power was invited to take part in the Greenwich Meridian Project by the UK's leading newspaper corporation, Times Newspapers. The company had recently taken over the sponsorship of the Meridian Line, London's historical landmark where Greenwich Meridian Time is measured from. The initial brief proposed replacing the existing brass strip, which

represented the time line with a significant intervention due to the Meridian's importance in the Millennium celebrations.

GLP's response was to form two rows of plasma television screens, set flush into the existing courtyard. The center line of the televisions would denote the line of zero degrees longitude. Each of the televisions would play a live satellite broadcast from a different time zone within each hemisphere. A service core was placed below the line of televisions allowing access for maintenance. GLP also proposed that a ski lift be installed to extend the line of the Meridian out over Greenwich Park to exploit the dramatic position of the observatory.

Greenwich Meridien Time
THE TIMES NEWSPAPER
ARCHITECTURAL COMPETITION
JUNE 1999

1

With reference in the introduction to the technique of sampling, GLP transposed this methodology to the project. GLP selected from an existing source, imagery, and form from the American architect, Neil Denari and applied this to the design of the ski lift.

GLP views this methodology as a completely legitimate operation. Just as the tenets of Modernism were adhered religiously to by those producing work under the banner of Modernism, GLP advertently reveal its sources. This paradigm of borrowing cultural references reflects the pluralism of its design. "To use this form appropriated from Denari for a structure placed on the Greenwich Meridian to celebrate its location was an obvious choice. Apart from its formal relation to the project, it is a cool shape in its own right," says Nic Clear.

The project concentrated around two of GLP's creative concerns: the integration of screen-based technologies within architectural elements to form an exquisite surface and the idea of appropriation of existing forms in "creative plagiarism."

previous page

1 The image of the service core that houses the TV plasma screens combine architectural construction lines normally used in plans to describe the foundation points within a perspective drawing.

this page

1 This detail illustrates the application of the sponsor's Times Newspapers logo onto the TV screens. The purpose of the TV screens is to relay live satellite broadcasts from different time zones within each hemisphere.

2 Bird's eye view of the pivotal structure of the project. The two TV plasma screens are placed on top of the service core. A countdown clock to the year 2000 is given a prominent position.

1

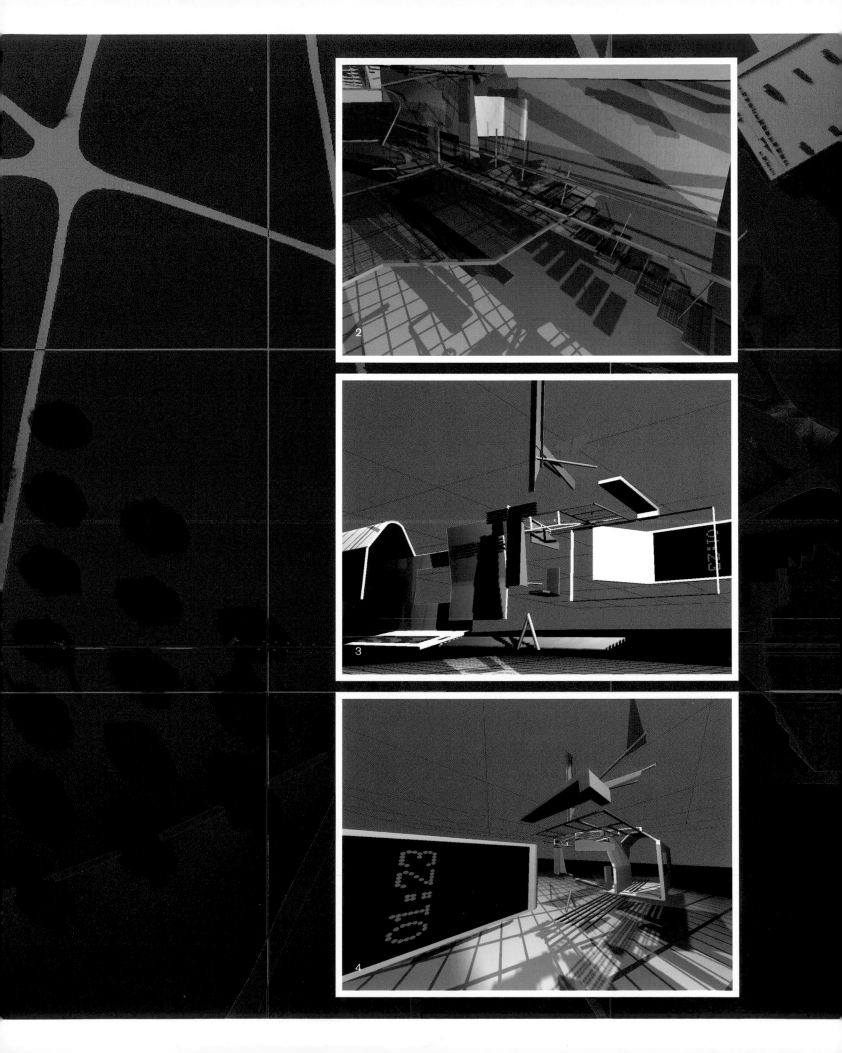

previous page

1 This aerial site plan introduces distorted perspective views of the north compass point. The area of the image representing the paths has been manipulated to introduce a sense of depth to what is normally a two-dimensional representation.

2 An exploded axonometric illustrates the staircase that leads up to the ski lift. The form of the ski lift has been taken from the folded topologies of Neil Denari's Interrupted Projections Installation at the Gallery MA.

3 & 4 Exploded axonometric drawings of the digital clock.

this page

1 This close up of the drawing's annotations projected in perspective are illustrative of GLP's ability to give graphic qualities a three-dimensional representation; in this case, with shadows cast from the numbers.

2 A detail of the architectural structure. The attention to graphic portrayal of color enhances the reading of the project on the page.

Marc Newson, the Australian-born designer now based in London, is notching up a series of commissions that show that his brand of sinuous design curves can be applied to restaurants, automation prototypes, wrist watches, and even a private jet. Joe Colombo inspired radii mixed with his love of surfing have manifested themselves in such designs as the aluminium Lockhead lounger and fibreglass furniture for the Italian manufacturer Cappelini.

In 1998 Newson was approached by a wealthy European entrepreneur, who wishes to remain anonymous, to design carte blanche the interior of his $42 million Falcon 900 B long-range jet. The client was familiar with various projects that Newson had designed, such as the interior of the restaurant Coast in London, Syn recording studio in Tokyo, and favoured Newson's sci-fi influenced furnishings. A prized commission for Newson, he decided to personalise the exterior of the jet and asked his old friend and collaborator Richard Allen, the graphic designer behind Mooks, the Australian clothing label, to collaborate on the project.

To design a jet is a stringent process. All interior fittings have to go through a rigorous testing procedure and comply with Federal Aviation regulations. The manufacturer of the jets, the French company Dassault, oversaw all of the design proposals down to the smallest details. Newson worked with the flight engineers based in Little Rock, Arkansas, where the Dessault jets are fitted out. Acquainting himself with the design parameters through consulting aviation journals, Newson's principal objective was to exceed on the luxury level and concentrate on making the cabin as comfortable as possible.

The exterior of the plane received it's own application of styling. Richard Allen decided to apply a giant dot screen that starts with a bold block of color as if the jet's cockpit has been dipped into a vat of silver paint. The dots then fade into white at the tail end.

For the main cabin quarters, Newson designed six plush black and silver leather seats with fold-out foot rests. The floor covering is a hand-woven silk carpet in a silver shade of gray with an organic stencil pattern in lime green. Black lacquer cabinets line the walls, which house fold-away tables and seats. Behind the main cabin area is a galley, small office, and two bathrooms (one for the crew and one for passengers). At the rear two rows of seating berths upholstered in black leather can be adjusted to provide sleeping space for two.

The finishing touches were added to the jet with the selection of design accoutrements to make on flight service a total design experience; "Grand Prix" cutlery by Achille Castiglioni was specified along with Alessi crockery. Newson designed his own range of glassware, silo-shaped so as to counteract the low center of gravity. The glassware was specially made by littala in Finland and is now going into commercial production. The finished design came to a grand total of $2 million dollars. Luxury comes with a price tag!

CLIENT
PROJECT DESCRIPTION
DATE

Marc Newson Private Jet
INFORMATION WITH HELD
AIRCRAFT INTERIOR
1999

1

2

3

4

1 Black lacquered cabinets conceal storage area, a galley, and small office, adding a degree of 1930's luxury reminiscent of the lacquered furniture of Eileen Grey.

2 Plasma screens can be folded out of the armrests. The hand-woven silk carpet was commissioned specifically for the interior of the jet.

3 Upholstered black leather seats fold out to form two single beds. Subtle lighting is concealed behind the white leather skin that is fitted throughout the jet.

4 Richard Allen's design for the exterior of the plane is influenced by the cabin windows. The jet was fitted out in Little Rock, Arkansas, with luxury seating at $20,000 a piece.

Established in 1978, the company Imagination, a huge creative networking hub which employs three hundred employees, has built its reputation on turning around conventional methods of brand building. Clients include the shakers on the global chess board, such as Ford, Guiness, British Telecom, and Ericsson. Imagination puts their expertise down to an ability to produce fluid design teams and resource allocation that is informal and organic.

Teams of architects, graphic designers, multi-media designers, photographers, lighting specialists to film directors, acoustic engineers and writers means that the scope of work they undertake is enormous. Commissions range from architectural projects, web site design, packaging, and product design through to events, exhibitions, retailing, and brand centres.

Imagination sits in the heart of London behind a six-story red brick facade, which belies one of London's most experimental interiors. Designed by Ron Herron in 1989, a former member of Archigram, the building incorporates two Edwardian warehouses and a street. Stretched over this area is a Teflon-coated tarp creating an atrium with aluminium and steel walkways linking the two buildings.

Conceptual design starts right at the beginning, with Imagination often becoming involved with the actual creation of a product in addition to the packaging and external product design. Imagination is deliberately nonhierarchical—only four people have formal titles. This leads to all involved feeling responsible for the success of a project and reduces the chance of conventional power struggles.

Journey Zone at the Dome

FORD
MILLENNIAL CELEBRATION EXHIBITION
DECEMBER 1999

Check in

1

The controversial Dome project was initiated by the Conservative government but taken under the wing of the Labour party when they came to power in 1997. Built to mark the Millennium celebrations, criticism from the media was targeted at the high cost of the temporary structure and its lack of curatorial direction. But slowly the Dome's popularity is incresing and the public and media are beginning to appreciate the shear scope and diversity of contemporary buildings concentrated under the Dome's roof.

The Dome's exhibition contents were split into sixteen zones each sponsored by a commercial sponsor. Imagination landed three of the zones; the Talk zone, the Journey zone and Skyscape. Imagination's role was to devise a concept that would steer the overall design and contents of the Journey zone. Ford motor cars, a long standing client of the company's thought it a natural progression to commission Imagination to design the zone.

Imagination took the concept of travel and interpreted it in its broadest sense. All modes of transport, from an historical perspective to an analysis of future proposed methods of transportation were exhibited. No expansive exhibition centred around transport would be complete without a critical look at the adverse effects of transport on the environment. The exhibition examined alternative modes of transport to the car and looked at governmental legislative policy on the future of transport.

To house the Journey Zone, Imagination's architects designed a three-story structure with a body of three tiered wings which dynamically project into the surrounding space. Pulled away from the main structure is the control tower with a steel structured staircase that wraps around the structure. Working closely with Imagination's architects, the graphic design team came up with process drawings that mapped the trajectory paths of travel. Various travel patterns such as flight paths and linear methods of travel informed the graphic panels and the dynamic structure of the building itself. The building has to fit amongst the giant pylon feet, each measuring four metres in diameter, which are used to support the Dome's roof structure.

1

2

3

this page

1 Interactive screens invite visitors to engage with the debate on environmental alternatives to present modes of travel.

2 Graphic panels present progressive concepts of environmental travel from pressure groups and transport related services.

3 The tensile cables attached to the pylons keep the roof material in tension. Imagination aimed to present a total experience through the execution of the Journey Zone.

4 Site work became a highly sophisticated operation with fifteen other sites being built

simultaneously and the restrictions of working round the existing structure.

next page

1 The exhibition provided an historical perspective on travel as well as providing a prognosis on travel in the near and distant future.

2 Text, structure and form are blended, providing an environment in which the visitor is subtly introduced to

the exhibits, without over loading the visitors with information or imagery.

3 Futuristic quotes of residents from projected groups, such as Global Community Future make comments on living in the next quarter of the twenty-

first century. Figure line drawings against silhouettes provide an animated sense of movement.

4 These linear trajectories complement the architectural structure and provide creative signs of how to move around the zone.

The external panels used to clad the building are N-16 halogen lights mounted onto extruded aluminium honeycomb sections normally used for high tensile structures. The panels are then bonded on to the structural frame. The cladding material is non-conductive but each light is wired onto a peg board then programmed to run different chasing sequences, to evoke an abstract sense of cars speeding down a motorway.

Internally the graphics are clear and communicative, influenced by the European graphics found in railway and airport information signage. One of the exhibition spaces looks at the design of transport interchanges, a burgeoning transport system as Europe increasingly breakdowns down its intangible socio-economic borders and physical transport links become increasingly important.

The control tower takes on the language of the ultimate Post-Modern space. Making reference to the generic spaces of airport lounges and transport interchanges where identity is defined by information and advertising screens. Imagination's zone captures this essence of non place and transports the visitor into a highly simulated environment where one can interact with video games and touch screen technology.

4

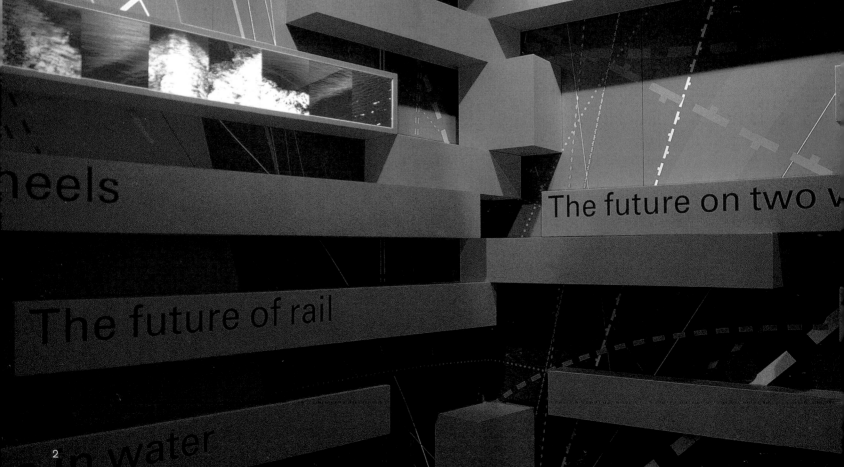

future journeys

millennium journeys

once-in-a-lifetime journeys

urban journeys

global journeys

innovative journeys

energetic journeys

1

heels

The future on two w

The future of rail

e in water

2

"...the fact that I live, work and ...n close to home. I can walk or ... most places and the pace of ... is quite leisurely." Tilly, 2027 –

ocal Living Future

"Nationality doesn't really matter anymore. Technology, especially the Internet, has shrunk the world." Manesh, 2025 – Global Community Future

"I like the fact that Britain stands on its own without Europe. I think we've got everything here we need for the future." Marnie, 2024 – Regional Focus Future

3

4

PRINCIPAL	KATY GAHREMANI	LOCATION	EDINBURGH, LONDON	YEAR FOUNDED	1994
	MICHAEL KOHN				

Two decades from now what will our homes look like? This is the proposition that Louise McKinney from the critical art and design practice Artery posed, inviting mixed design teams to dream up a concept of what homes in the year 2020 will look like. The international competition invited entries that would "produce an intelligent building which describes a new interdisciplinary blueprint for the future of domestic architecture."

The winning scheme the HangerHouse™, responded by providing an inventive and integrated design approach, radically redesigning the traditional housing form, function, and uses of the "domestic realm."

The ambitious scheme drew on the revolution in e-commerce, basing its concept on a customised "pret-a-habiter" home that could be bought from the web. Various technological components were integrated into the scheme, such as an intelligent nerve centre that governs everything from heating to electricity, monitoring waste expenditure and an intelligent bathroom named "the body wash" that simultaneously washes, weighs and performs a series of health checks, ultimately recommending a diet of a proposed low calorie shopping list.

The winning architects, Katy Ghahremani and Michael Kohn, in collaboration with a diverse creative team from management consultants to product designers, selected Navyblue.com, a team of web site designers, to create the integral component, the web site design for the HangerHouse™. Navyblue.com have already gained experience in this field, working together with a mainstream housing contractor Millar Homes who are beginning to introduce high volume housing onto the market that can be specified from their website address. Navyblue.com created the point of sales information, a catalogue of electrical white goods right down to the finer details of mortgage specifications for the commercial housing company.

The collaboration of both teams was an ideal harnessing of creative resources. The combination of the HangerHouse™ team, which had not worked in the field of on-line design, but upon which the success of the HangerHouse™ depended and Navyblue.com who rose to the challenge of translating ambitious design concepts into a tangible system has produced an innovative project for the future of housing procurement.

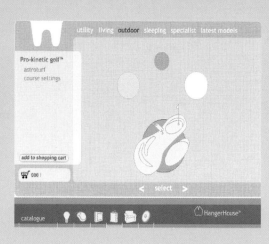
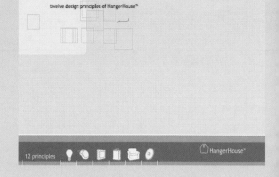
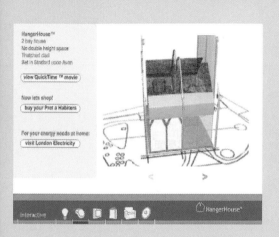
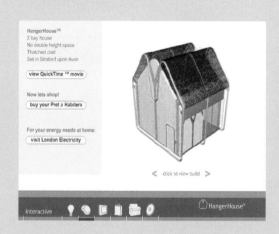
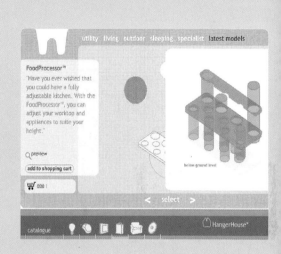
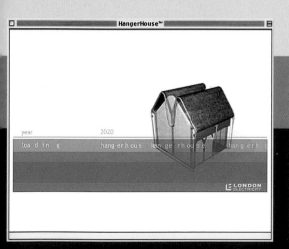
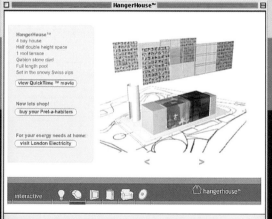
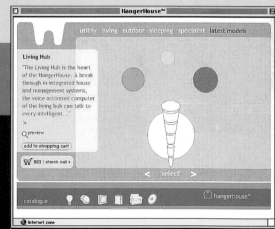
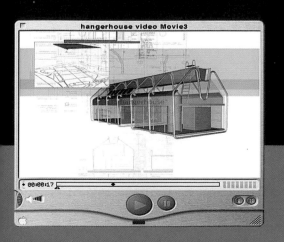
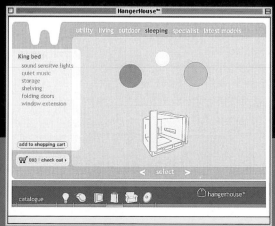

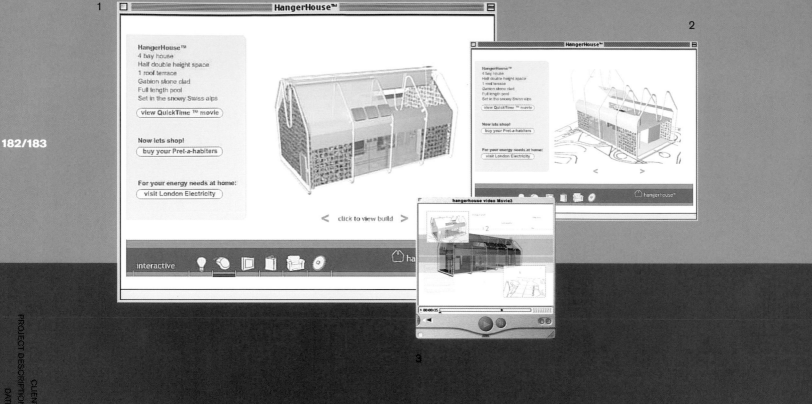

CLIENT
PROJECT DESCRIPTION
DATE

HangerHouse™

DAILY MAIL GROUP
COMPETITION FOR THE HOUSE OF THE FUTURE WITH WEB-SITE DESIGN
APRIL 2000

1 Image of the screen interface illustrating the catalogue on-line.

2 Easily recognisable graphic symbols help the users to access the areas in the site that advise on energy consumption, furnishings and construction details.

3 The HangerHouse™ video movie aims to communicate the concept of sustainable, efficient and fun housing made accessible through the Internet.

4 (and following pages)
Lounging in the interior with the pret-a-habiter modules and the cylindrical living hub, which can be personalised to the owners own energy requirements, in the background.

5 The isometric computer drawing demonstrates a six bay house with clip-on lap pool and photo-voltaic panels.

5

4

The HangerHouse™ is a skeleton structure that can be appropriated to suit the individual needs of each owner. Its flexibility in terms of size and structure means that it can be dressed up or down depending on the life-style requirements and future technological advancements, without compromising its own design integrity. The design's only common element is the frame which resembles the typical shape of the domestic pitched roof. This standardised element is selected from the web, each buyer specifies the quantity of bays and selects all their own elements, from cladding and photo-voltaic panels to the specification of roof terrace, lap pool or patio.

Internally, the prospective home buyer can select from the pret-a-habiter modules. They provide compact and efficient furnishings for sleeping, eating, preparation of food and

bathing, as well as more specialist activities. And if the urge to redecorate may arise the pret-a habiter modules can be sold back to The HangerHouse™ Company and upgraded to keep up with improvements in technology.

Navyblue.com set out to design a website that would hand over the control of house design to the buyer. An interactive web site allows the user to select from the range of structural components and design their own customised house. A quick time video demonstrates the falling into place of all the components, enfranchising the user into the realm of house design.

Navyblue.com were adamant that the selection process of build your own home would be told with as little text as possible, instead clear and straight forward graphics would be used to communicate the concept.

6

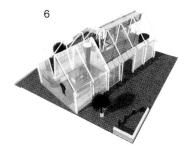

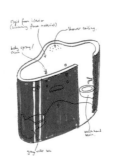

1

6

hangerhouse video Movie3

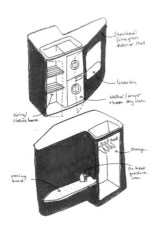

2

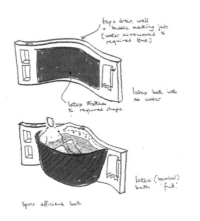

3

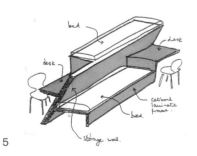

4   5

7

8

9

10

1 HangerHouse™ illustrates intgrated design response to future housing concepts.

2 -5 The sketches show initial design ideas for the prêt-à-habiter modules for utility and washing requirements.

6 The video has a voice over guiding the user through the design of the HangerHouse™.

7 Sections and technical diagrams explain the construction details combined with the three-dimensional image of the house demonstrating the main components slotted into the frame.

8 This still taken from the movie illustrates how the lap pool fits into the hanger type frame.

9 Smart Pans, an example of one of the futuristic labour saving cooking devices designed by Seymour Powell, enables the user to download cooking instructions from the Internet, direct to the pan.

10 An illustration of the different types of cladding panels that can be specified. In this case Gabion stone cladding, a favourite of architects such as Herzog and De Meuron, and glazing panels.

DIRECTORY

Marc Newson Ltd. and Richard Allen
Heddon Street
London W1R 7LE England
T: 44(0)171 287 9388
F: 44(0)171 287 9347

The Designers Republic
The Workstation
15 Paternoster Row
Sheffield S12 BXT England
T: 01142754982
dr@thedesignersrepublic.com

Fat
116-120 Golden Lane
T: 44 (0) (207) 171 251 6735
London ECIY OTC
fat@fat.co.uk

General Lighting & Power
112-116 Old Street
London EC1V 9BD England
T: 44 (0) (207) 171 490 7975
the.general@virgin.net

Graven Images
83a Candleriggs
Glasgow G1 1LF Scotland
T: 44 (0)141 552 6626
F: 44(0)141 552 0433

Imagination
25 Store Street
London WC1E 7BL England
T: 44 (0) 20 7323 3300
www.imagination.co.uk

Ben Kelly Design
10 Stoney Street
London SE1 9AD England
T: 44(0)171 378 8116
F: 44(0)171 378 8366
bkduk@dircon.co.uk

Lippa Pearce Design Ltd.
358a Richmond Road
Twickenham TW1 2DU England
T:44(0)20 8744 2100
T: 44(0)208744 2770
mail@lippapearcedesign.com

Met Studio
6-8 Standard Place Rivington Street
London EC2A 3BE England
T: 44 (0)171 729 4949
F: 44 (0)171 729 1638
amanda@metstudio.oo.uk

Marc Newson Ltd. with Richard Allen
Heddon Street
London W1R 7LE England
T: 44(0)171 287 9388
F: 44(0)171 287 9347

Orb Design
Urbanstrasse 116
Berlin 10967 Germany
T: 49 30 61286 166
F: 49 30 61286 167
orb.serve@snatu.de

Pentagram
11 Needham Road
London W11 2RP England
T: 44(0) (207) 171 229 3477
www.pentagram.com

Softroom
34 Lexington Street
London W1R 3HR England
T: 0171 437 1550/44 (0) 207 4371550
softroom@softroom.com

STIP
System Typography Integrated Program
Lange Haven 80 NL-3111 CH
Schiedam, Holland
T: 31(0)10 473808
F: 31(0)10 4737408
info@blh.nl

Tonkin Architects Ltd.
1 Goodsway
London NW1 1UR England
T: 44 (0)171 (207) 837 6255
F: 44(0)171 837 6277
tonkin@zoo.co.uk

Traast and Gruson
Lange Haven 80 3111 CH
Schiedam, Holland
T: 31 1104265438

24/seven
83A Geffrye Street
London E2 8HX England
T: 44(0) (207) 171 729 9194
F: 44(0) (207) 171 729 9193

Author's Note

Corinna Dean trained as an architect at University College, London. She practiced in Berlin before returning to London where she currently curates exhibitions that examine cross-disciplinary design activities as well as explorations into how design and architecture respond to advances in digital technology. She also contributes regularly to a wide range of publications, such as *The Architects' Journal*, *The Architectural Review*, and *Deutsche Bauzeitung*. Her research into regeneration of under-developed areas has taken her to the Gaza Strip in Israel, Nicosia, and Beirut.

corinna dean